MUSINGS OF A WORKMAN

ON

THE PAINS AND PRAISE

OF

MAN'S GREAT SUBSTITUTE.

BY

THOMAS BROWN, CELLARDYKE,

AUTHOR OF PRIZE ESSAYS ON "THE SABBATH,"
AND ON "THE BRITISH WORKMAN."

———

"Which things the Angels desire to look into."—*Peter.*

———

ANSTRUTHER: LEWIS RUSSELL.
EDINBURGH: J. MENZIES.
1861.

PREFACE.

WERE the various materials that constitute
society as accurately examined, defined, and
classified in our systems of social economy, as
are the materials which constitute the globe in
our systems of geology, it would be found that
the class denominated the " British Workman "
is as distinctly separate from the degraded
masses that occupy the under levels of human
existence, and disturb and distress all grades with
their depravity, as any of the other more elevated
classes are; and that those higher classes of
society, in proportion to their numbers, contribute
to the magnitude and virulence of that depravity
at least an equal share with the humble workman.

We, therefore, demur to the process by which
philanthropists of the present day, in their gene-
rous schemes for elevating the masses, generally
manage to include the workman in the same
category with the victims of crime and depravity;
and would apply the same remedy to the one as
to the other.

The workman's position in the social system is
of all others the most useful and important; and,
inasmuch as his resources are in himself, it is the
most independent; and as he accepts and acts
upon the original conditions of existence, without

evasion or subterfuge, it is of all others the most
honourable and upright, though not the most
honoured.

It is, however, true that, from the irrepressible
energy with which every department of business
is prosecuted in this country, his physical powers
are often subjected to a ruinous amount of
exertion ; while his mental faculties suffer a pro-
portionate amount of neglect, or are prostrated
beneath the pressure of physical toil, and the
difficulty of rendering its proceeds adequate to the
daily wants ; so that his intellectual and moral
being are often in imminent danger of being
carried away in a current of materialism, that
derives its highest pleasure from the indulgence
of debasing sensual enjoyments, and not from the
higher instincts of his rational being.

With more sympathy than penetration, this has
been sought to be counteracted, by affording him
access to some of the more refined,—though fre-
quently very frivolous sources of physical gratifica-
tion,—which, when embraced, often proves simply
a new form of bodily exertion, equally exhausting
with his accustomed avocation, without awakening
one dormant faculty in his rational being.

It is admitted that there are some employments
in themselves physically unwholesome, and that
others are prosecuted in such ungenial circum-
stances, that much physical advantage would be
derived by the frequent enjoyment of uncontami-
nated air, or other similar appliances. There are,
also, perilous pursuits, on land and ocean, by

which human life is curtailed, or materially shortened. In all such cases, where the evil cannot be averted, the smallest alleviation of course is not to be despised in either of those cases.

But the general rule of labour, and its disadvantage in this country, is, that it is limited only by the power of exertion, or the endurance of the physical constitution; and, consequently, that the whole being is often thereby crushed into the aptitudes and appliances of a peculiarly constructed, self-acting engine of labour, instead of being fostered into a healthful, rational existence.

If we turn to those engaged in intellectual pursuits, we find that in them the over-taxed mental faculties are, as it were, instinctively relieved and invigorated, by arousing the suppressed physical power to activity in athletic amusement and recreation, which restore the combined functions of mind and body to a healthful equilibrium. Doubtless mere cessation from study would relieve; but it would not counteract. The cure is found in the unrestrained activity of the physical system producing a counterpoise to the over-wrought mental.

It is, then, a plain analogical deduction to affirm that, while the workman may be relieved by periods of cessation and amusement, he is not materially improved thereby—that the equilibrium of his constitution can only be restored by furnishing him with energetic mental employment and recreation; and that the creditable imitation of some lovely landscape, the execution

of some stirring musical composition, the working
up of some intellectual idea, or a thousand other
mental pursuits, uniting physical rest with mental
activity, inspiring a dignity of sentiment, a consciousness of self-respect and moral worth, which
will convey a refreshing influence through the
heart and affections, is vastly more elevating
and effective than all the physical appliances so
much patronised and advocated at the present time.

Give the workman a mental existence by
moderate culture in his early youth, and in
riper years let him have an agreeable rational
hobby to work out; then he feels himself in a
position of dignity which he would not be easily
induced to dishonour or abandon.

The following pages are not expected, nor
intended, to introduce the humble author into
the arena of fame; nor are they intended to add
to the literature of the country. They are pre-
sented simply as an illustration of the above
propositions regarding the British Workman,
having already served their original design as the
mental recreations of a working man. They are
unblessed by the refinement and polish of educa-
tion; and the object of their publication will
have been attained if they should in any measure
contribute to the exposition and promotion on
the part of the philanthropist, and to the adoption
on the part of the workman himself, of a similar
course of mental activity and recreation, in order
to counteract the wear and tear of every-day
labour.   THE AUTHOR.

THE GREAT SUBSTITUTE:

HIS PAINS AND PRAISE.

CHAPTER I.

ARGUMENT. —Invocation of the Divine Light that
Inspired the Revelation of God's Gracious Designs
towards Man.—These Designs and Purposes, known
only to Himself, arrest the attention of Angels
from other Glorious Themes.—The Essential Glory of
God. — Its Display in Creation, near and remote,
Exceedingly Attractive. —The Subject proposed In-
finitely more Amazing.—Attempt to Trace, first the
Humiliation, then the Glory of the Redeemer.—Divine
Guidance again invoked.

COME ! Inspiration of Seraphic Song !
Whose energies awoke those countless harps
Harmonious, pealing in ecstatic strains
Of swelling rapture, 'midst the glorious spheres
Of Paradise above ! Inspire my song ;
Light—Love impart, and numbers fitly fram'd
To utter thought sublime, by prophets once
In heav'nly cadence sung, and human phrase

A

As best might reach the wayward ear of man ;
Revealing high designs, and mighty deeds,
Beyond the spacious sphere of seraph thought,
To curious study prone, and deep research,—
Form'd in the Triune Mind, ere Time was known,
And there enclosed, within the secret folds
Of Wisdom's inaccessible recess ;
Till, from the depths of vast infinitude,
Perfections new, evok'd by human wants,
Should burst in glory on created view.

 Amazing theme ! that shoots its dazz'ling beams
Athwart the regions of angelic ken ;
With higher import fraught, and richer fruits,
Than aught besides that draws their raptur'd
 thought,
And stays its buoyant flight, while on the wing·
Of holy contemplation and delight,
Amidst the wonders crowding into view
From pow'r creative, or sustaining might ;—
From these to turn, by impulse deeper moved
To earnest study, and perchance descry
Some radiant outlines of another sphere
Of energy divine ; in features new,
With brighter glory gorgeously arrayed,
And deeper wisdom curiously inwrought ;
By all perfections wondrously combined,
Intensified, to more mysterious deeds,
Impressed more deeply with infinite skill,—

To know its nature, apprehend its worth
And high design, as, to the finite view
It upward rises to development.

Permission full lured the angelic thought
To ample fields, where contemplation bright
Might roam for ever in perpetual bliss,
O'er boundless splendours of Omnipotence,
Stor'd up in vast resource, within the grasp
Of the Supreme ; amidst the sacred shades
Of light ineffable, yet unapproach'd
By penetration less acute and clear
Than eye divine ; where bliss essential rolls
In sov'reign glory, purity, and love—
In ceaseless solace in its own regards ;
Yet symbolis'd, reflected, and displayed
In fitting measure, to the finite mind,
That lowly bends before th' imperial throne,
And to perfection nearest can attain ;
By whom those emblems are distinctly seen,
And import trac'd, and high attraction felt,
Infusing life more copious and sublime,—
More true devotion,—still a wider range
Of clear conception of the Holy One,
And conscious feeling of his loved embrace.

Or, when by fiat of creative pow'r,
A wond'rous universe emerg'd from shades
Of dark intangibility, and rose
Array'd in bright perfection's purest garb,

A glorious thing of majesty and grace,
To shed it's lustre o'er intelligence ;—
Then, Thought gigantic spread its ample wing,
Brac'd and compacted for the daring sweep
Of broad Creation's measureless domain ;—
Nerv'd by perception keen, and reason strong,
And penetration clear, and firm resolve,
And ardent love, and aspiration pure,
To scrutinise, and know, and upward soar
To unsearch'd regions of almighty pow'r,
And rest amaz'd on pinnacles of Truth,
All radiant with benignity and love,
Where Wisdom, lavish of infinite wealth,
Has strewn all being with her precious gifts ;
Nor tarries there ; but, with profound amaze,
Surveys the texture of the blazing spheres,
So nicely balanc'd in imtrodden space
Around the mansions of the Holy One ;
Adorn'd with new-lit rectitude and life,
To gild the portals of eternal day
In unexpress'd magnificence and light,
And symbol forth, from sphere to sphere beyond,
The bliss and glory resident within.

  Or, speed afar, out to unnumber'd worlds,
Which wheel unerring in their varied course,
Trac'd in the vast infinitude of space ;
To reach those further orbs, whose dawning light,
From climes of imperception dim, have brav'd

Their per'lous voyage to the glorious main
Of boundless being, fraught with tidings clear
From the lone outskirts of immensity :
Where reigns exhaustless energy and care,
Paternal love, and goodness unimpair'd,
Device acute, and wisdom rolling deep,
And bright, and pure, in distant solitudes,
As in Creation's teeming thoroughfares—
These to discover, and their wonders scan,
Admire their beauty, symmetry, and gifts,
And in them all to trace the bounteous hand
That gave them wants, which He himself might fill.

Thus, to behold a universe of light,
Near, or remote, all glorious in the beams
Of bliss, imparted by creative pow'r ;
On each bestow'd with open, lavish hand,
All fresh and fragrant from the source Divine,
As if each one the sole recipient were
Of Heav'n's o'erflowing holiness and love.

Yon flick'ring speck, in murky distance pois'd,
'Midst sombre shades of deep obscurity,
Far from the busy haunts of kindred life ;
Out in the gloomy wilderness of space—
Revolving round its unobtrusive course
As first impell'd ; beyond the feeble range
Of human science or angelic thought ;
And, as it speeds, irradiates the praise
Of Him, whose pow'r and wisdom knit its frame

In adaptation to its tireless race,
And trac'd its orbit on the mighty void.
Though isolated from all kindred spheres,
And far remote, in regions of neglect,
Where undisturb'd obscurity presides,—
Unknown, unnoticed, till light's weary steed
Reveals its being 'mong created things,—
Yet Wisdom there in undiminish'd strength
Has spread its plains and rear'd its mountains high,
And fill'd its stores with goodness manifold ;
While over all Heaven's unexhausted care
Sheds the effulgence of benign regard,
To nurse devotion, love, intelligence ;—
Imprints the seal of ownership thereon,—
Th' imperial stamp of holiness and truth,
To make it worthy of its high design,—
The full completion of a universe,
Whose every sphere, near or remotely pois'd
Throughout the vast infinitude of space,
Might all combine, like harp of many strings,
To swell the glory of Jehovah's name.

Oh ! glorious combination ! Boundless theme
Of finite contemplation and research,
On which enraptur'd seraphs love to dwell !
And feed the cravings of increasing light
And holy wonder, admiration, praise !
While they survey, as in a mirror bright,
The perfect wisdom and consummate skill,—

The sov'reign goodness, holiness, and pow'r,
And vast resource all resident in Him
Who, undiminish'd, rear'd those mighty piles,
With impulse throbbing for their glorious race ;
And sent them forth into immensity,
Teeming with life, and in perfection cloth'd,—
Diversely group'd, in orderly array
Of prominence, and shade, and lab'rinth deep,
And vale, and spacious plain, and bow'ry mead ;
Amidst whose anthems of perpetual praise
Divinity reclines, and calls them good ;
Unfolds His being, attributes, designs,—
Displays His glory, and imparts His bliss
Throughout creation, to remotest date,
And draws it upward to His dwelling high,
In adoration and enraptur'd praise.

Yet from creation's unexplor'd domain,
And all its wonders never to be scann'd,
Angelic thought, as if unmov'd, withdraws ;
Perchance by less attraction sway'd ; they turn
From things inferior unto higher themes
Of marvellous design and mighty deed ;
Converging inward from the distant range
Of bold discovery, to ponder deep
Into the secrets of profounder skill,
And wisdom more sublime,—more intricate ;
Deeds more amazing,—pregnant with results
More glorious to Jehovah's holy name,

And to the creatures which His hand has form'd,
Than the vast fabrics of creative pow'r.

While we, by light drawn from the sacred page,
Attempt the bold design,—to find our way
Within those depths profound, where seraph eye
With wonder and astonishment grows faint,
And droops amaz'd,—O, may the Guide Divine,
Great Fount of Light,—the Third of One, inspire,
Uphold, and guide our perilous attempt
At more than seraph flight!   Give wisdom clear,
And pour fresh oil into the lamp of truth ;
That, as our thoughts with trembling awe descend
The dread recesses of infinite wrath,
And felt demerit, wretchedness, and woe,
By man incurr'd,—and in his stead endur'd
In all its fearful magnitude and weight
By his Great Substitute, the Sinner's Friend.
Or, as with hearts elate we upward rise
In contemplation to the vast results
Of glory won, and majesty display'd,—
And love reveal'd, exerted, and enjoy'd ;
Till now unknown beyond the mind Divine,
Our spirits gross may catch th' etherial flame,
And upward soar upon the golden wing
Of Truth Divine, towards the sacred heights
Of love and glory,—where in triumph reigns
The great Redeemer of the human race.

While mortal pinions seek celestial spheres,

To range those sunny climes, of high acclaim
And anthems loud, to rich redeeming grace ;
Casting our humble tribute of the heart
In grateful adoration, 'midst the peal
Of bright seraphic universal song,
To Him ascrib'd—the purchase of his woe ;—
That deeper insight we may thence acquire
Into the depths of that mysterious love
Which mov'd to deeds amazing and sublime,
And wak'd the wonder of celestial hosts.

CHAPTER II.

———

In time primeval, when Jehovah's pow'r,
Led by the goodness of His sov'reign will,
Prone to felicitate, and propagate
Thro' countless streams the riches of the Fount,—
Hung round th' imperial throne with matchless
   skill
Unnumber'd spheres, absorbent of his care,
To share his riches and exalt his name ;—
'Twas then that earth, deck'd by his bounteous
   hand,
Bright as a dew-drop in the blushing morn,
Rang'd 'mong the myriads of resplendent orbs,
And sallied forth on her untrodden course,

Fresh in the vigour of her countless charms.
Her bosom heav'd with full felicity,
And all her regions buoyant were with joy ;
Her plains were teeming with exuberance ;
Her valleys laden with luxuriant fruits ;
Her terrac'd mountains fragrant with perfume ;
Her forests melting with melodious song ;
Her glassy ocean to quiesence hush'd,
And on her placid bosom hov'ring cloud,
And hill, and forest seems again retraced,
Reflecting back the glories on her shed ;
Or, sportive dang'ling with the flowery coast,
In gentle ripples on the margin lav'd ;—
On all her scenes tranquillity diffus'd
Intrinsic beauty, happiness, delight.

　Mov'd by the impulse of unessay'd pow'rs,
Which in exertion found supreme delight,
All sentient being triumph'd in her gifts—
The strong and weak ;—the rude and gentle join'd
In union unalloy'd ; with varied pow'rs
And faculties endow'd, yet all combin'd
Into harmonious unity and peace.
The groves resounded with unceasing song ;
The zephyrs paus'd and caught the mellow tide,
And bore it upward in a flood of joy,
To be infus'd with heaven's ecstatic strains,
And thence return in copious show'rs of bliss.
The breezes chaunted hymns symphonious ;

And rivers play'd upon the silv'ry harp
Of ocean's placid wave.   All life was praise ;
All sound and motion felt the impulse pure,
And, sweetly drawn, spontaneous swell'd the
   strains
Of exultation in Almighty praise ;
And echo bore the melody on high
Through balmy ether to th' imperial ear
Of Great Jehovah, whose paternal smile
Complacent rested on the infant world.
Those smiles were life, and happiness, and joy,
Which virgin Nature quaff'd, and sweeter grew,—
More pure and lovely ;—more expressive too
Of the perfections, attributes, and aims,
Whence she deriv'd her beauty and renown.

   Oh ! 'twas a glorious world ! rich in the wealth
Upon it lavish'd by the hand Divine ;
Bright with the traces of infinite skill,
Which through undying ages might have sung
In hallow'd tones the glory of its Lord.
Yet there was nought amongst its varied scenes
And tribes diversified, of kindred mould
And fitting texture, to receive and hold
The influx of Divinity most pure.
No reservoir wherein benevolence
Might pour the essence of felicity
To the relief and solace of itself,
And blessed be in pouring out its bless.

Hence man of earth was form'd; with wants
supply'd -
From thence,—of sentient life,—combin'd with
gifts
Intelligent,—akin to higher spheres ;—
Rays from the altar of the Holy One,
To light him to the skies, and draw him there ;
Capacity to search the mines of truth,
And scale the heights of knowledge ; to inquire,
Reflect, investigate, compare, and know ;
To feel emotion, sentiment, design ;
Produce, enjoy, reciprocate, delight ;
To sympathise and blend with kindred hearts ;
Attractive draw, or to attraction yield,
In closer union with superior thought ;
Or rise enraptur'd on devotion's breath
Into the regions of seraphic joy,
To drink celestial ravishment and bliss.
   Man—thus exalted ! Deputy of Heaven !
Bright image of perfection ! Honour'd sire !
Though latest form'd of all terrestrial things,—
In guilt a novice, in experience
And true felicity most erudite,—
First trode elastic on the new-made world.
In ev'ry step was majesty and grace ;
In ev'ry thought was purity and love :
His foot own'd kindred with the lowly earth—
His mind rose upward to celestial spheres:

Both met in him ; things visible and gross ;
Enclasp'd the unseen in refin'd embrace.
He, part of both, in each a perfect thing,—
Connecting link that near'd the earth to Heav'n.
  'Twas thus man walk'd upon the flow'ry earth,
And on its verdant mound bent low his head,
Enshrin'd in dignity and honour high ;
From things beneath to cull the essence pure,
As fitting incense to the throne above.
Then chaste Humility drew near, and cast
Her robe of meekness round him, and entwin'd
Her heart in his, as spirits can co-mix ;
And taught him homage to the great I Am.
Emotion woke to consciousness, and drew
Unfeign'd devotion from his secret heart,
In thrilling strains of fervent gratitude,
Refin'd in essence as the rich perfume
That wafts its fragrance round Jehovah's throne,
And melts immortal beings into bliss.
These, borne to halls of Paradise, inspir'd
A louder peal of high exultant joy
Through climes celestial.   Rapture fleeter flew
On messages of love to human kind,—
Long'd more intensely to be near, and view
The spirit-flame so brightly burn within
So gross a vessel as the human frame.
    Strange sight it was ! Who would not turn
    aside

To see the fire, fann'd by the Spirit's breath,
Encompass and pervade the lowly bush
With unconsuming flame ?—and read thereon
The glorious doings of the great Supreme ?
  Man was the high-priest of the new-form'd globe.
He led the choir.   All Nature breath'd response
In accents pliant to his upright will ;
Calm placid Eve and sober Night retir'd
To placid meditation.   Blushing morn,
Pregnant with smiles of gladsome day, approach'd
On golden wing.   The fragrant dews awoke,
And deck'd the sward in bright transparency ;
The leafy herbage, cloth'd in glowing charms
Of luscious fruits and variegated bloom,
Embower'd unnumber'd shrines ; and Silence hung
In solemn invitation, breathing awe
And calm tranquillity.   The zephyrs shed
Celestial fragrance upon bow'r and shrub,
And pond'rous forest, and luxuriant plain,—
Inducing sweet devotion in all tribes
Of living things, prone to express in song
Or joyous gambol, strength, agility,
Instinctive pleasure in their new-found gifts.
With kindly mien the lordly lion crouch'd
Beside the harmless lamb ;—unus'd to blood,
The tiger gamboll'd with the helpless kid
In friendly tenderness ;—the wolf, unskill'd
In cunning, was unfear'd ;—the eagle stay d

The eager impulse of his rav'nous flight,
Subdued to peace by all-pervading love ;—
The greedy vulture knew not all his craft ;—
The owl then social was ;—the raven tame ;—
All own'd submission, and were prompt to yield.
The laggard sped—haste curb'd his fiery steed ;
The weak and mean, by gentleness preferr'd,
Receiv'd an honour'd place, and fill'd it too,
At Nature's hallow'd shrine. No sullen brow,
Or haughty sneer, with look contemptuous, shed
Invidious feeling through those sacred courts ;
No feign'd pretence or hollow " stand aside "
Obtain'd an audience 'midst the varied throng,
Far less pre-eminence,—or sought to sway
The tone and texture of their tribute pure.
All as they could—each by his own device,
In import, attitude, and humble zeal,—
As form'd and furnish'd by the sov'reign will
Of perfect Wisdom for the high design,—
Combin'd and fraternis'd with one accord,
By various effort, and with various means
From common source deriv'd, to raise on high
A cloud of incense on the wing of praise,
And true devotion, gratitude, and love,
From universal Nature to its God.

CHAPTER III.

THUS Time began, and with it man's estate,
Of sweet subjection to the highest good ;
Life there was nurs'd. It was the breath of
    Heaven,
Fraught with felicity in him infus'd ;
His only test content but to be blest ;—
The golden chain of love ineffable,
That binds celestial principalities,
Thrones, powers, dominions, every grade
Of lofty being, to unfading joy,—
Let down to Earth, to draw it up to Heaven,
By Time environ'd,—as with fleecy cloud
The flow'r is shaded from the noon-day sun,

B

A genial bow'r of quietude, apart
From ecstacy too bright, where, unabash'd,
His knee might bow, and living voice ascend
In audible expression of his joy.

Admiring hosts converging paus'd to view
A thing so strange,—a union so unique :—
Matter ennobled by intelligence,
And yielding tribute of celestial growth ;
Emotion deepen'd as they, pond'ring, thought
Of record ancient, dimly writ within
The page of stern resolve, or trac'd obscure
Some feeble outlines, full of grave import
To Sov'reignty supreme, and dubious fate
Portentous pending o'er the human kind ;
And they had seen deep movings strangely urge
Essential glory, as forecasting ire
With pity struggl'd for supremacy ;
And they had seen the undeclar'd resolve
Of Sov'reign will, assume an awful tone
Of consultation, ere by crowning act
The fed'ral head of human kind was formed.
The high behest, in majesty announc'd,
Not unresolved, deliberation chose
In solemn council of the Triune Mind,
That augur'd vast results.   These well they knew,
And sought to fathom, while they ponder'd deep ;
But o'er their vision deep humility
And strong amazement spread their dark'ning folds.

Oh ! had man's prowess and integrity
Prov'd faithful to the lavish care of Heaven,
Then his estate of high felicity,
Environ'd round by rectitude and truth,
Had been secure ; repelling bold assaults
Of hellish wiles, insinuations, pride,
As burnish'd steel repels the futile shaft
That speeds to pierce the throbbing heart within.

    Or had the foe, curs'd spoiler of our race,
Made bootless search for earth's serene retreat,
Sunk in th' untravers'd gloom that yawn'd between ;
Then malice foil'd, reluctant, unappeas'd,
Had coil'd insatiate in his lurid den,
To gnaw his rage in envy and disgrace.

    Then wrath to man had ever been unknown,
Conceal'd 'midst slumbers of oblivion,
While its dark frown and pestilential curse,
Like wall of fire far in the distance rais'd,
Had ever guarded all terrestrial things
From the approach of the perfidious foe.
Earth without blemish, and without a pang
Had bloom'd in beauty of perpetual spring,
A fit retreat where Godhead might retire
From government supreme, yet govern all,
To be solac'd with fealty of earth.
And man, of sorrow unappris'd—by guile
Untouch'd, unstain'd—had quaff'd perpetual bliss ;
Pure and devout his songs of gratitude

In fragrant odour, on elastic thought
Uprising, had infus'd a deeper tone
Of melody through Heaven's triumphant strains ;
The ladder, too, 'twixt spheres of earth and heaven,
Had stood unshaken through all coming time,
For Angel transit to th' abodes of men ;
While their communion, flowing ever on
In endless streams, had chang'd the earth to heaven.

But Malice saw, and hatch'd the hellish plot
That crush'd the glory of man's first estate,
And quench'd his short-lived honour in disgrace.

Time scarce had spread her young expanded
          wing,
To sweep the circuit of her daily course,—
Earth scarce had felt the glory of her task
To foster human kind for nobler spheres,—
When Heaven's arch-foe beheld, with envious eye
And hate malignant, his rejected bliss
Upon another, humbler race, bestow'd.
Fir'd by despair, resentment, and revenge,
Quick from his quiver flew a deadly shaft,
Unfalt'ring hurl'd, that pierc'd her to the core ;
Smooth-tongu'd temptation reached the human ear,
And spread his wiles before th' unguarded eye ;
Frail inexperience listen'd—was beguil'd ;
Doubt, discontent, insidious crept within,
Engend'ring pride, ambition—fatal guests :
And man, oblivious of his high estate,

With all its honour, dignity, delight,
Paus'd, dallied, tasted, and was overcome.
A shock flashed through his being, and diverg'd
Through all creation, like a pang of death ;
The light and lustre of primeval bliss
Were in a moment quench'd, and he was lost.
Truth was ignor'd, and Rectitude was crush'd,
And Virtue fled precipitate to Heav'n,
And Reason stood oblique, and Knowledge fail'd,
Save loathsome insight into visions vile ;
And all Divinity within collaps'd
Into a wither'd relic of the past ;
While conscious degradation, guilt, and shame,
Now made him cower in terror and dismay.

   And this is Death !   Life's aspirations hush'd !
The pulse of Love is still !   The vital stream
Of pure affection, impulse, and desire,
Is stagnant now !   The upright will
That made obedience, privilege, and joy,
Has turn'd aside !   The voice of praise is mute—
Its hallow'd themes forgotten and despised ;
The keen desire, and appetite acute,
For heavenly manna, and celestial springs,
And all the functions of activity,
That but a moment past in vigour sprang,
Elastic as a sunbeam, to the call
Of love and duty ;—prostrate as the grave,
And loathsome, too, as that abhorr'd abode.

Yes, it is Death ! in most revolting form ;—
Not mere extinction—that were bliss compar'd ;
Not wip'd away, like an uncomely stain
Dropt on Creation's page.   Annihilation ?   No,
That cannot be, beneath th' Almighty's eye ;
He, in Himself, His glory, works, designs,
Assail'd, no diminution can sustain ;
All still remains ; but in abandonment,
And foul corruption, breeding ghastly woe.
Knowledge remains, and memory acute,—
Sensation vivid burns, and strong desire,—
And aspiration strains spasmodic out,—
Anticipation keenly reaches forth,—
Reflection, too, to ruminate is prone,
But, broken loose, and to confusion hurl'd ;
Chaotic mass ! whose combination serv'd
To fill experience with dread misery !
A filthy pool, where all vile sentiments,
Ideas, tastes, might welter unrestrain'd ;
And conscious guilt pervading, spread the gloom
Of retribution, dire as very hell !
And jealousy creeps in, and fulsome pride,
(Unseemly harlot in a fallen world,)
With all her train of flatteries and crimes ;
And sullen discontent, ambition, hate,
Reproach, and dread, recrimination, ire,.
And green-eyed envy ; callous selfishness,
And grasping avarice, find a ready place ;

And falsehood tortuous wriggles into sway,
With perfidy behind, and scowling scorn,
Impiety profane, and lawless thought :—
All pregnant evil ; and concupiscence
Pours like a flood into the empty soul,
By goodness left, perdition to sustain.
  Oh ! it was Death ! unlike the gentle touch
That reins the jaded steed when at the goal,
Shuts out the steam, and leaves the engine still ;
The friendly hand press'd on the weary pulse,
That toil and labour hushes to repose.
The sever'd twig expires,—and is no more.
Beauty retires from the once smiling cheek ;
The clouded eye and rigid sinew blend
In close conjunction with their kindred earth ;
But no disturbance the lone grave invades,
Save the commotion of the nauseous worm ;—
The noble structure huddl'd out of sight—
And all is o'er. Not so th' apostate soul ;
It dies a living death ; beyond the reach
Of dark oblivion. No consuming force,
Inducing dark nonenity, is felt
Within the precincts of the soul undone ;
'Tis dread experience ; terrible influx,
Unmitigate, intense, of untold woe.
  'Twas Death ! tremendous in its dire results
Of universal carnage ; like the crash
Of a huge avalanche, that overwhelms

With utter ruin all within its sweep ;
Blood-stain'd ambition, drunk with human groans,
That goads her vot'ries in delirious sport
To slay their myriads for a paltry whim ;
Inspires to tame exploits ; inflicts a wound
Of mean pretensions, weigh'd with that foul deed
Which swept a race entire from life divine.

   Death to himself ! How foul ! Base suicide !
To spurn a life replete with happiness,
And throw it back in the great Donor's face,
As thing of naught ! in utter disregard,
And proud contempt, of such a paltry boon ;
Yet, since he choose it, he must now endure,
With firm resolve, the penalty involv'd ;—
His hardihood may brave the fatal choice,
Or, unavailing, ponder with regret
His reckless madness, 'midst perpetual shame.
Yet one reflection ('tis a common one)
May blunt the sharpness of his self-reproach,—
May still remonstrance, and the conscience hush,
" The wrong is his, the consequence his own."
But here such palliation is unknown ;
For *all* he stood, his failure was their fall ;
Their fate in his, for life or death was bound,
As he comported, and for them procur'd—
So in him they must suffer or enjoy.
Oh ! then, what need to walk with wary steps,
And humble trust upon the mighty arm,

When life so num'rous, and so precious, too,
Dependent hung upon his rectitude.
Self-murder !—Cowardice supreme seems light
With guilt so heinous, in the balance weigh'd :
A race undone, and to perdition hurl'd,
By the custodier of their future weal ;
Within the refuge of Almighty pow'r,
Oblivious of the high imperial will,
And duty's hallow'd claims, and filial love, —
The innate yearnings of parental care,
That ever intervenes to shield its own
From threaten'd danger in the hour of need ;
Oblivious, too, of good already his,
And rich experience of complete delight,
And full conception of the boundless store,
Secur'd by promise, to fidelity.
To him how precious ! and for all how full !
These for himself in madness he ignores,—
Ignores them, too, in name of all mankind,—
Disclaims, denounces, and repudiates,
In impious disobedience to his God.

    Nature recoil'd, and reel'd beneath the stroke,
As reels the victim at the fatal stab ;
As shrinks the mortal frame in ev'ry nerve
When outrag'd law or rampant tyranny
Rolls the dissever'd head into the dust,—
So dread amazement seiz'd on ev'ry clime,
And stricken earth grew dismal with the shock ;

Her virgin robes, wherein she joyous met,
With verdant gladness, her appointed lord,
In ghastly gloom hung like a funeral pall;
Her bosom, teeming with all precious fruits,
In essence stor'd to lavish upon men,
And nourish sentient life, refus'd to yield
Its vital strength, those treasures to mature;
Her youthful verdure wither'd to decay,
And o'er her beauty stalk'd sterility.

   Death reign'd ev'n here, and sent its vapours
    forth
From stunted wood, and rank obnoxious herb,
And marsh, and swamp, and putrefaction foul,
To wrap existence in continual doubt,
Full of suspense, uncertainty, and dread,
Sustain'd by shrivell'd plants, and seeds
Penurious, yielding but a felon's fare
To the base culprit, wrung with anxious toil.

   Yet, in this death oblivion was refused,
To hide the shame of things inanimate;
Extinction cannot touch heaven's meanest works,
As if their being were a gross mistake;
The theatre of man's vile apostacy—
Polluted earth, its burden and disgrace
Must be sustain'd; its mission to perform,
Subservient bow beneath the high designs,
Mysterious, undivulg'd, of heaven to man.

   Ponder, my soul! Conceal it as you may,

By carnal pleasure, or consuming care
About the passing int'rests of an hour ;
The brief accommodation time supplies
To meet the cravings of thy mortal frame,
Until the heart has wove a callous crust
Of hard obtuseness to the dread of sin,—
Has rais'd a bulwark of oblivion
Against th' unwelcome importunity,
And urgent clamour, conscience may excite
About provision for a future state.
Hell stands in need of no locality,
No horrid regions 'neath the sway of night,
With adamantine bars, and molten flame
Tempestuous surging, to ensure despair,
And prove damnation a reality : .
It burns within, in consciousness of guilt,
And sin prevailing, enmity to God,
And stern exclusion from his loving face ;
It is a living death, that ever gnaws
Upon the heartstrings of the deathless soul,—
Becomes more hopeless as it burrows deep
Into the secrets of its memories,—
More greedy grows, devours with keener zest
The foul corruption that engenders woe,
And makes it everlasting.

Not man alone, nor earth with all her tribes,
Stunn'd with the shock apostacy produced,
Recoiled, astonished at the fatal deed ;

Celestial hosts, in consternation, paus'd
At strange dissonance in the melodies
Of Heavenly bliss.   Nor were they long in doubt,
Ere rapture seem'd less copious, as from earth
A wail of anguish, like a requiem, rung
Far in the distance, over man laid low ;
Swift in the wake of triumph it arose—
Struck on the jasper walls of light, and bore
Astonishment within.   Seraphic harps,
With solemn awe and dubious thought, grew mute ;
And glory seem'd less glorious, appris'd
Of Paradise assail'd ; and insult shot
Against the bulwarks of Omnipotence ;
Grave contemplation hung her head in grief,
As echo bore symbolic tidings up,
Through pendant clouds of ecstacy and lights,
To inner mansions, where on highest throne
Sits Majesty Supreme, that man had fallen.
Repuls'd beneficence less bounteous seem'd ;
In smiles less bright, dispens'd immortal gifts ;—
Goodness infinite, set at naught, withdrew
To pour her treasures on a holier clime ;
And Love withheld her ill-requited care,
And stay'd her floods divine ; Complacency
Held back her smiles ; and Pity spread a veil
Of pure regret, o'er the less loud acclaim,
That rush'd elastic inward to the Throne,—
For Peace retired, and Rapture fled from earth,

And Innocence serene, and Peace, and Joy,
And all the handmaids of Integrity,
Repell'd, outrag'd, fled from proximity
With deed so flagrant, and with guilt so foul,
To find a home in more congenial climes.

CHAPTER IV.

UPON the earth the Great Jehovah stood,
Strict guardian of the universal code,—
The high criterion of all rectitude,—
With vindication arm'd ; its injured Lord,
In dignity sublime, and judgment clad,
And human form, as oft ere now he stood
In sweet communings with the lord of earth.
Legions unseen, obsequious bend around,
With praise cognisant by His ear alone ;
Degraded Nature into silence sunk,
Crush'd in the travail of her sore disease,
And paus'd suspicious, while its mighty Sire
Once more appear'd a visitant to man.

" Adam ! where art thou ? whence this om'nous
   change
That keeps thee absent from the fragrant grove
(To thee familiar spot) in wonted hour
Of holy meditation—in the calm
Of dewy eve ? from highest heav'nly themes,
Inviting thought, and wooing thy regard,
So justly claimed by tenderness and love,—
A love that sparkles from the budding bough,
And fragrant flow'r, and mellow luscious fruit,
That radiant sparkles in all sentient life,
Inspires the joyous exultation felt
In new-found instincts, to be gratified,—
That longs to touch thy soul and waft it up,
On wing of ecstacy, than winds more fleet,
To be absorbed, and ravished in thy God.

  Why flag the earnest longings of thy heart
To reach communion still more intimate,
And more resemblance to my image pure,
Which in the highest, can no higher rise
Than likeness faint, to essence unapproach'd,
Where thy desire more vigour may attain,
To drink more deeply in celestial joy ?
Why mute the song of praise ? why fails thy voice
To raise the hallow'd strains of innocence
Up to Jehovah's ever open ear,
When comes the silence of the closing day ?

  'Twas never so before ! My voice unheard

No joyous answer to thy Maker's call !
'Tis tenderness itself that audience seeks,
And condescends, permission to demand,
To beam complacency Divine on thee ;
To pour a higher bliss, more thrilling joy,
And raptures more intense, into thy heart ;
To gird it with a holier bond of love,
More unreserv'd confiding trust in Me ;
To fill thy mind with more exalted views,
And fuller knowledge of thy happiness ;
To understand, appreciate, and feel
Still stronger impulse towards heav'nly things ;
More strength to wield, appropriate, requite
Increasing honours, still in store for thee.

 'Tis tenderness extends her open arms
To clasp thee to her breast ; that would relieve
Her pent-up feelings, in more copious streams,
Beyond thy power to bear ; that thee invites
To ope the sluices of thy swelling heart,
With ecstacy surcharged, that so the tide
Of love, and gratitude, and praise, may gush
Into the ocean whence it was diffus'd ;
To walk around and mark the bulwarks strong
That circles all thy hope ; and drawing nigh,
To blend in one, assimilate, and bind
Thy present being in probation plac'd
With promis'd glory in celestial spheres,—
Midst whose delights probation is unknown,

Where fervent love and pure felicity,
Without condition, tenant ev'ry soul,
And radiates out from ev'ry shining face,
By Heaven's decree, and sweet experience seal'd,
To full presistence in eternal life.

 Where art thou, Adam ?　What dark deed is
  thine ?
Why is yon sky obscur'd ?　Why hides the sun
In sorrow's weeds, e'erwhile suffus'd with smiles ?
Why sickens life ?　What makes her countless
 streams
Subside in bleak sterility ?　What taints
Her vital tide ?　What blights the bloom of youth,
And steals insidious into all her pores ?
Whence spring incipient pain, aversion, doubt,
To mar the harmony of sentient tribes ?
Why trembles earth beneath the tread Divine,
As if its Maker had become its foe ?
How stands thy compact with thy gracious Lord,
By test so simple held, so easy met,
That thy convictions must approve its terms
Enough to prove allegiance, nought to wake
The faintest feeling of imposed restraint ?
Is all upright with thee ? or else, alas !
From filial duty hast thou swerv'd ?　A foe
To God, thy Judge !　Dost thou repugnance own
At His approach, who reads thy secret soul ?
Does conscious guilt aversion interpose ?

Does creeping fear, ill understood dislike,
Restrain the ardour of thy wonted love,
And make thee laggard in the trysting hour,—
Becloud the glory of My matchless love,
Impede its influx, check its copious flow
From Me to thee, as when the fragrant dews
Subside, portentous of the pending storm,
As yet unwitness'd in thy peaceful home !
Why low'rs suspicion on the face divine ?
And why distrust within the human heart ?
What intervenes ?   An enemy to both,
That breaks the tender cord, till now so strong,
Excluding thee from converse with thy God.
   Oh, grevious change is here !   The hidden
     depths
Of thine own heart unloos'd, disorganis'd,
Revealing guilt, from disobedience sprung ;
Whence lawless passion, inclinations vile,
And hateful lusts, and all uncleanness, rise
In base rebellion 'gainst thy righteous Lord,
And drive perdition through thy ruined soul.
How dim the gold ! how chang'd the purest gold !
Thy honour lost !   The mighty, how debas'd !
Estrang'd from Me !   Recoiling from my sight,
As if concealment were within thy reach ;
Renouncing my authority ; with it
The rich provisions of infinite care,
And boundless love, and purposes of grace,

And gifts most precious, partly in thy hand,
And amply treasur'd up, to be increased
With thy increase, through roll of future date :
All cast away, rejected, and despis'd,
As worthless things, deserving no regard.
At variance with thy God, and with thyself,
When worth adher'd to thee ; with what is good,
And most beloved, most sought, desir'd, and priz'd,
As most conducive to enhance the worth
And lasting pleasure of the finite mind.

Where art thou, Adam ?   Now confederate
With Heaven's apostate foe,—with thine own foe,
Who envied thee with deep malignity,
Design'd to fill the place in my regards
His pride renounced, by thee renounc'd as well ;
By him entic'd, his willing abject slave,
Shut up to wrath, and out from love divine ;
From hope excluded, and from finite aid,
And wills it should be so—no faint desire
Disturbs thy deep insensibility,
That arm more potent would stoop down to save."

So God.   So His vicegerent too.   In doubt
And troubl'd cogitation, self-accus'd,
At His tribunal man in shame appear'd,
Unwilling drawn by consciousness of guilt,
That dragg'd him forth ; for terror interven'd,
And tried to hide him from the searching eye.
The culprit must ; nor will confession wait,

Though parried by excuse.   By fatal spell
The wretched felon owns his heinous crime,
While in evasion courting a retreat
From piercing holiness, that search'd him through,
And plac'd his naked sin before his view.
His Judge was Justice.   Truth the fact declar'd ;
Omniscience witness bore, and testified
To gifts bestow'd, his uprightness to guard ;
All Nature witness bore.   It would not hide,
But, like a lep'rosy, ooz'd out in spots
Incurable, that could not be conceal'd ;
And shame bore witness, forc'd acknowledgment,
From bootless efforts to elude the glance
That frowning pierc'd into the secret soul,
And saw the poison drop, with malice fraught,
Into the crystal stream, unrecognis'd,
While vile desire insatiate held the sway,
And made indulgence sweet, though at the cost
Of highest honour, rectitude, and peace ;—
Ev'n yet, but faintly felt, less understood,
While its demerit seem'd in balance hung,—
That saw the pair, like wounded birds, retreat
Within the lab'rinths of the leafy shade,
Unable to endure each other's gaze,
With the barb'd arrow fest'ring in their breast,
Inducing weakness, stupor, and alarm ;
Beheld the poison course through all their veins—
O'er all their being—into all its depths—

Infusing blindness, stupefaction, death,—
No faculty exempt, no pow'r unstain'd.
'Twas ruin universal and complete ;
Saw it descending, like a putrid stream,
From age to age, and forth to ev'ry clime,
Quenching all life, of ev'ry grade and hue,
Drawn from the earth, or rooted in the skies.
Omniscience scann'd, in all its magnitude,
The loss sustain'd ; the glory cast away ;
The sore disaster on the race entail'd
By base divergence of their fed'ral head ;
Could sound the depth of the unfathom'd pit,
And knew the fierceness of devouring fire,
The gnawing worm,—the ever living death,—
The endless anguish, unsupportable,
Involv'd in that dread fate,—Perdition.

Oh, that men saw it, in its native guise,
Deform'd, as seen from heights of holiness,
With Wisdom's vision clear, in light of Truth
And stern reality, while yet escape
Is possible ! The mighty aggregate
The Judge beheld, and melted at the sight ;
And tender Pity wept ; Compassion yearn'd,
In silent sadness, o'er the havoc made ;
Relentings deep sway'd the Imperial will ;
And Vengeance paler grew,—his fiery car
More tardy seem'd,—to vindication sore
Reluctant drawn,—with appetite less keen ;

And Mercy hung upon th' uplifted arm,
And bar'd her bosom to the whetted sword;
For man she pled, as she ne'er pled before,
For higher being, till success was hers;
Her copious tears mov'd Justice to delay,
And grant a precious season of respite.
Then Wisdom ancient, cloth'd in love divine
And majesty severe, mov'd by resolves,
Matur'd in council of th' Eternal Will,
Pregnant with deeds of deepest mystery,
And sacrifice unmatch'd, and vast device,
And pow'r supreme, such as Almighty God,
And He alone, could form or could divulge;—
These he propounded in arrest of death,
In vindication of insulted Law,
And reparation of Imperial wrongs;
Hell stood aghast, and all her legions fierce
More dismal grew in disappointed rage;
Death gnash'd his adamantine chain, and grinn'd
In avarice most horribly; and Sin
More monstrous and detestable appear'd.
   But Love rejoic'd; and sweet Compassion sung
Triumphantly; while thus Jehovah spake:
   "O Jerusalem! O Jerusalem!
How oft with cords of everlasting love
Would I have drawn thy children to my heart,
Within the refuge of my mighty pow'r!
Ev'n as the hen her helpless tender brood

O'ershadows with her wings, so would I shield
Thy feeble offspring in my boundless love
From the assaults of thy malignant foes,—
But thou in scorn hast turn'd thy heart away.
How shall I leave thee, base as Admah's plains?
How, as Ziboim, give thee up to wrath?
How shall I open all its crimson floods,
And with its waves o'erwhelm thy rebel soul?
How thee abandon to entire dismay?
How thee consume with anguish and despair?
Oh, thou art wretched! but its very depth,
By thee unsought, though not by thee eschew'd,
More precious makes thee seem—more dear to Me.
I would not thy destruction, but thy life;
My bowels turn; all my repentings move;
Thy death no pleasure to my nature yields;
Thy restoration rather would Me please.
With double aim the fatal shaft is arm'd
At God most High, through creature most belov'd;
'Tis malace aim'd at my prerogative,
And must be foil'd, to Satan's utter shame.
Yet die thou must, for Justice claims its due;
'Tis seal'd already in thy mortal frame;
Death festers there, with virulence intense,
Until that frame, the instrument of crime,
Enfeebl'd by its inroads, shall succumb
To weakness, degradation, labour, shame;
To abject bondage, weariness, disease,—

Till years congeal the vital tide within,
Elastic once with immortality,
Unloose its cords, and crush its various parts,
Like thing rejected, in th' ignoble grave ;
For dust thou art, and shalt to dust return.
Eternal death awaits ; but Mercy pleads ;
Nor does she plead in vain ;—this understand,
The woman's seed shall crush the tempter's head ;
But, not unscath'd, shall victory achieve."

CHAPTER V.

ARGUMENT.—The Effect of Adam's Sentence.—Degradation of his Moral Faculties.—The Loss Aggravated by former Happy Experiences.—The Disorder in his Mind.—The Blight on Creation.—The Enmity of the Inferior Creatures.—The Spared Sinner a Subject of Curiosity to Angelic Beings.—The Consequences of Sin on the Affections.—Alleviated by the Introduction of Hope.—Mankind Practically making Adam's Choice their own.—Despair.—Is Merited by us, as well as Entailed upon us.—The Folly of Discussing, instead of Accepting, a Way of Escape.—Apostate Angels had not such Offers as are Rejected by Men.—The Difference a Subject of Wonder to Angels.—Their Adoration of the Divine Sovereignty.

FROM Eden's happy bow'rs respited man
Was driven, with brand of degradation fixed
Indelibly upon his aching heart ;
Not death immediate, as the law implied,
But death commuted, as the doom reveal'd,
And on conditions for a time delay'd ;
Enough impos'd, whence he could estimate
With some precision what the whole must be,—
The bitter fruits apostacy produc'd,
And feel the contrast to those choice delights

Which Paradise supplied : as men yet feel,
By sad reverse, the good so oft despis'd.
Had the reflection but to him remain'd,
That his disaster was result of fate,
For which he was no match,—that to his trust
He still adher'd,—how would the thought, retain'd
Amidst his wreck of fortune, have infus'd
A soothing influence o'er his prostrate heart !
But nought remain'd—nought left him to assuage
The dreary desolation.   Memory,
Alert and vivid, gloomily review'd
Perfection lost, with all its glorious train
Of pure desires for ever realis'd.
Knowledge, expanding, nursing tastes refin'd,—
Increasing wisdom, holiness, delight,
The will directing, to exalting joys,—
The inclinations, appetites, desires,
Like loving spouse, by sweet attraction drawn,
To reason's noble sway, in homage just,
Producing bliss, akin to Heaven itself.
These she review'd with sorrow and remorse,
And brooded sadly o'er the sore reverse,—
O'er days departed,—joys for ever gone,—
And blasted hopes,—and friendships broken up,—
And honour lost,—and highest worth debas'd,—
And confidence abus'd.   Oh, what a trust !
The universe contains no parallel.
To generate a race, ordain'd to praise

In accents new the Great Creator's name,
Amidst the myriads that surround His throne,—
That trust betray'd, and every impulse crush'd
That mov'd to hallow'd themes! Now superven'd!
The will estrang'd, and prone to seek its good
Among the husks of sense; imperious grown,
Impatient of restraint, or law, or rule,
Beyond itself. The inclinations vile,
Deceitful bent towards indulgence gross;
Knowledge to evil drawn, and wise therein;
Reason perverted, and desire debas'd;
Hope, love, and fear, drunk with those poison'd
    streams,
Bred misconception, agitation, doubt.
Thus tumult, strife, and all extravagance
Assum'd the sway, gave law, and was obey'd,
And him enslav'd to ev'ry lawless lust,
Who anxious onward to the future gas'd
In dread suspense of what might him await.

All Nature on him frown'd; its varied course
Antagonist became. Death seem'd inscrib'd
On every thing, and witness'd to his shame:
Upon the waning leaf, and fading flow'r,
And furious storm, and parched wilderness,
And stunted shrubs, and blighted wither'd fruits,
And elements array'd in wild hostility,
Loos'd from their bonds of just subserviency
To human wants, and Heaven's gracious care.

The bestial tribes, involv'd in the foul blight,
Refus'd subjection to a prostrate pow'r ;
Dishonour'd and debas'd, ferocious turn'd,
And on each other prey'd voraciously,
Then fiercely frown'd in emnity on man,
Who grew more feeble as his foes increas'd.
Guilt made him powerless where he might have
    reign'd,—
A sneaking coward when no harm was near ;
All objects seem'd invested with the pow'r
To consummate anticipated woe.

Man so respited was a problem deep,
Exciting curious thought and strange surmise
'Mong hosts celestial, vigilant to catch
A deeper view of wisdom unrestrain'd,
Through Sovereign grace display'd,—a channel new,
And open only between Heav'n and earth.
Strange combination in a finite soul !
Of wrath the subject, but of mercy too ;
The curse inflicted coursing through the veins,
Polluting all within, while he remains
Uncrush'd beneath the weight, yet helpless there ;
Hope still sustaining, without pow'r to free ;
From Heav'n debarr'd ; Hell yawning underneath !
Akin to both, and yet by neither claim'd,
A race in equipoise, within the range
Of restoration, in apparent death !

    'Twas desolation—not abandonment ;

His native pow'rs and faculties remain'd
Entire and active as in Eden's bliss ;
But, jumbl'd in disorder, without rule
To guide their motions in a virtuous course ;
Perversion universal overspread,
And deep infus'd into the secret heart,
Inflicting loss, He only can pourtray,
Whose thought capacious can unfalt'ring sweep
The glorious circle of perpetual joy,
With all its springs of measureless delight,
And bring the sum within the potent grasp
Of comprehension, and survey it there.
See the bereavement, and revulsion dire,
And dread negation, when those living springs
Were in a moment from their course revers'd,
Inflicting anguish, terrible to bear ;
Alike mysterious to the mental grasp
That has not trode the fathomless abyss,—
Drunk its despair, its agony, and shame,
And felt its darkness horrid and profound
Engulph and deluge the perverted soul.

By right of purchase, such the human fate.
In part awarded ; much held in reverse ;
Enough inflicted to transform the race
To very demons, and the once fair world
Into an hell of anarchy and crime.

But 'midst the desolation Hope appear'd,
And could be gather'd from this obvious fact—

Converts all present good to bitter gall,
And binds its victim to distress and grief,—
What must it be, where ev'ry thought is fire,
And sense remorse, and sight dismay, and sound
The wail and anguish of unutter'd woe?

  Despair! What seraph nearest to the throne
Of high Infinitude, whose mighty grasp
Encircles things immense, and thoughts profound;
Whose sage experience, ancient and renown'd,
Soars highest 'mong the high,—or downward drops
To depths of terror, near the outer spheres
Of dread abandonment, and yet returns,
Unscath'd, to revel 'midst ecstatic bliss?
Oh! who is he the horror can describe
Of irremediable rejection? Who
Can penetrate the solitude and woe
Contain'd within one moment of despair,
Far less conceive it rolling on, and on,
For ever, with accumulated strength,
While being is prolong'd?

  Pause, oh my soul!
The doom was thine; your conscience tells you so;
Thine the inheritance of guilt and woe,
By right inherent,—ratified, confirm'd
By deed and doing of thine own free choice;
By act consenting to the first foul deed
That brought thee low.   Thus often you've
  approv'd,

And claim'd the portion Adam chose for you ;—
By him unseen, it was his error then ;
To you, most clear, it is your folly now ;
By perfect right the curse is all thine own ;
By heirship thine—and thine by purchase too—
Award most just—by thy demerit earn'd.
A twofold claim is thine ;—reciprocal
The bond that seals perdition as thy due,—
By parentage convey'd, and render'd sure
By mutual fitness, and attraction too.
Thy title indefeasible. Appeal
Is totally in vain. Avoidance vain.
Denial most absurd. Forgetfulness
Is folly mad. Discussion out of place.
Admit the fact, and ponder the results,
That render worse impossible, and makes
Escape and safety an eternal boon.
Let hatred quibble at the glorious means,
While any means are worth ten thousand worlds ;
Let madmen struggle for an empty name,
Or evanescent pow'r, or sordid wealth,
And petrify their souls in the pursuit,
As if perdition were too doubtful else ;
Let wisdom lead thee to a nobler course.

What ! would'st thou rivet the infernal chain
Of unbelief upon thy soul, as if
Afraid damnation else were insecure,—
Add tenfold aggravation to thy guilt

D

By base rejection of a safe escape ?.
In stubborn pride, would question, and deny,
Dispute, discuss, or else forget the fact
Of your demerit ! 'Tis the strongest proof
Of its existence, and your danger too.
Give Mercy praise, and praise infinite love,
Give God most high the utmost of your praise,
That all its woe is not already yours.

 All have not fared so well. When angels
  sinn'd
Respite rais'd no obstruction to their doom,
And Mercy found no argument to urge,
Nor willing daysman to avert their fate ;
Then Justice swift unsheath'd his whetted sword,
Bright in the terrors of the Lord, and drove
The rebel hosts to vengeance and despair,—
Crush'd with a stroke their foul audacious pride,
Subversive of authority supreme,
And the diffusion of His sov'reign love,—
Wip'd off the insult offer'd to His throne,
In vengeance dire and woe unutterable ;
And round supremacy's almighty seat,
And round the temple of seraphic praise,
And round ineffable delight, and peace, and
 love,
A rampart rear'd, of holiness aveng'd,
And law unsullied, which none might assail
And hope to live,—debarring aught unclean

Within the precincts of His holy place.
 All have not fared so well ;—their fate and
  .yours
How wide apart ! To them 'twas ire divine
Unmitigate, pour'd on audacity ;
To you 'tis sov'reign pity, as the dupe
Of restless malice, enmity, deceit.
 These fates diverse struck the seraphic throng
With strange surmise and study intricate,
Into the depths of infinite design,
Whence issued doom, so much unlike ; where
  love
And wrath were each so vividly display'd ;
In deeper awe they yielded to the might
Of light essential, drawing them within
The lowly refuge of humility,
While love enclos'd them in the ample folds
Of holiness unstain'd, and hid them there,
Safely conceal'd from the consuming storm,
O'erwhelming fiends, and low'ring upon man.
Before His throne they cast their shining crowns.
And hid their faces with their golden wings,
To each they whisper'd, but to the Supreme,
In loudest peals of high ecstatic praise :—
" Thy works, how great and marvellous, O Lord !
Just judgment are the pillars of Thy throne ;
Thy doings all are righteousness and truth ;
Thy name who would not glorify and fear,

Of his apostacy in colours more distinct,—
His vile contempt of Heaven's o'erflowing good,
By him enjoy'd, and treasur'd up in store,
In rich abundance for his future race,—
His utter weakness to retrieve the loss,
To know, or will, or understand the good,
Or choose the path of rectitude and life
Amidst conflicting claims for his regard,
And strong allurement, view'd through medium
    false,
And moral sense to evil ever prone.
    Oh ! how can life subsist in such a state,
Where desolation universal reigns ?
How cancel guilt, or restitution make,
For law outrag'd and sov'reign love ignor'd ?
How purge the stain cast on created things ?
What blood, save the trangressor's, can efface
A blot so foul, and make all pure again,
As in primeval days ?   What can subdue
The dark repugnance of the human heart
To pure delights and intercourse with Heav'n ?
Can high Omniscence overlook the past,
And in oblivion hide its dire results ?
That cannot be.   But were it even so,
Can the Eternal stoop so very low ?
Or if He can, is there a power in Him
To re-infuse His essence in the heart,
And cause it beat responsive to His will ?

Yet if he cannot, must infinitude
Sustain reverse at puny creatures' hands ?
The rich effusions of benevolence
That in the source essential glory feeds,
And ever urgent to diffuse its streams
Of full luxuriance over being all,
Repuls'd at first, within the courts of light,
By foul ambition, enmity, and pride ;
And now rejected by the human race,—
Where find recipients of its precious store ?
A fitting outlet for its copious tide,
Where Love, by blessing, may *itself* enjoy,
And, by expression, be itself express'd ?

Angelic beings have their fill of bliss ;
A greater strain on their supreme delight
Would overpow'r them with excess of good,
And bring disaster on their high estate,—
For finite vessel can sustain no more.

What then ! shall earth, form'd for a meet abode
To the recipients of o'erflowing love,
Where good infinite might its treasures pour
In varied richness and intensity,—
As Wisdom's hand can aptly touch, and trace
On moral being, nurtur'd for a course
Of glorious progress upward to the goal,
Where high Infinitude himself resides,—
For ever nearing, never yet attained,—
Shall it remain an unproductive blank,

Amidst the glory of the universe?
A standing proof that malice may succeed
At least to thwart, if not to overcome,
The mighty doings of Omnipotence,—
May mar His high benevolent designs,—
Obstruct its flow, repress its bright display,
And blast the objects it resolves to bless.
Shall the Almighty tamely bear repulse,
Without device to shame th' audacious foe,
And turn his shafts of malice on himself?
To spoil the spoiler of His handiwork,
Shall He permit th' effulgence of His love,
That beam'd complacent on the human race
In copious floods of rich felicity,
To be for ever shrouded in the gloom
Of vengeance unappeas'd, and ever due?

   A mystery this no finite mind could solve!
Then what device, ripe in the mind divine,
Sway'd His procedure towards fallen man,
And cloth'd His ire in soft compassion's garb—
Unwonted features in the Holy One?

   Yet man was spar'd! This solitary fact
Hush'd many anxious doubts, and render'd man
A problem to himself and all besides.
Angelic penetration vainly sought
Some faint analogy, wherewith to sound
The deep designs Compassion had matur'd,
To place the sinner where none else had been,—

Above the region of complete despair,
Yet far beneath the sweet abodes of peace.
What strange device, conceal'd in love divine,
From all obstruction free, remains unknown ;
Can Honour, Law, or Justice vindicate,
From man apart, or in him so sustain'd,
That the infliction may not him destroy ?
Can calm the fierceness of infinite ire,
And o'er its tempest bridge a passage safe,
Where erring thought, in aspirations weak,
May humbly reach a welcome in the skies ?

  Is substitution possible ?   If so,
And one might bear demerit not his own,
Oh ! who has prowess for the mighty task ?
Who wields the pow'r to woo the rays of life
From its rejected source ? to bind anew
The human heart with more enduring love ?
Or having pow'r, where is the willing one,—
With high regard for majesty assail'd,
And deep compassion for the human race,—
To undergo the overwhelming sense
Of all demerit, that men might escape ?
Expose the bosom that ne'er knew a pang
To all the horror of unutter'd woe ?
The will and courage to confront and brave
Th' uplifted sword, with indignation keen,
And drink the fervour of its hottest ire,
And turn its vengeance into melting love ?

Can substitution fully satisfy
Eternal justice ? right inflexible ?
And Truth maintain untarnish'd as of old ?
Produce obedience to the sov'reign will,
Whose fiat girds the boundless universe
In one adjusted, pure, harmonious whole,
So that its parts, united or detach'd,
In ev'ry section, vast, minute, remote,
Or near the mighty Mover of its varied frame,—
May image the perfection that presides
In undiminish'd majesty o'er all ?
Diffuses truth, and rectitude, and life,
Throughout all being, upon all inscribes,
In blazing terms, as with a pen of light,
" Who keeps shall live, the breaker thereof dies."

To human kind, can substitution prove
A safe retreat against infinite wrath ?
Prove warnings vain, and threatenings also vain ?
And turn the curse aside, already pil'd
Like a huge mountain on his prostrate head,
With its dread poison fest'ring in his veins,
Deep, virulent, incurable as death ?

Oh ! can infinite wisdom uncreate ?
Solve the mysterious problem long conceal'd ?
Reveal an antidote to man's disease ?
Remain intact in all perfection high,
Unchang'd custodier of untarnish'd truth
And righteousness supreme ? on which may rest,

Seraphic trust, exempt from ev'ry doubt,—
Th' acknowledg'd source of all supremacy,
Jehovah ever glorious in his works,
Recipient of all praise, devotion, love,
Font of all excellence, for ever blest,—
While guilty rebels bow not to his sway ?
Has Wisdom a reserve of deep device
Yet uninscrib'd upon creation's page,
Withheld from finite mind, e'ernow unseen
In sov'reign dealings with intelligence,
By which to wrest it from the hopeless sphere
Of contradiction, where ev'n boundless pow'r
Arrested, cannot stultify itself,
And range it 'mong things possible with God ?
Can this be done, ev'n by Almighty pow'r ?
Can highest knowledge, wisdom most acute,
Achieve a triumph, soaring far above
The highest surmise reason can attain ?

  Creation, teeming with amazing proofs
Of might untrammelled, wisdom unperplexed,
And penetration nothing can deceive,
Yields no solution, no analogy,
To guide inquiry to development,—
Through all her spheres no parallel is found
Whereon to rest a probability,—
No kindred deed, whence deep research may
    trace
Some indications of such strange results ;

Light springs from light ; unclean from unclean
   springs ;
And guilt from guilt : to find in error, truth ;
Or in rebellion, peace ; in enmity,
The living seeds of happiness and love ;
Extremes united, blended, harmoniz'd,
Till life with death in loving embrace dwell ;
The law, that all created things upholds,
And reproduction rules, pronounces vain.

   All providence, exuberant of good
And blessing manifold, in fulness shed,
And utmost measure, upon creatures all,
From the archangel to the crawling worm,
As each has space and function to contain ;
No precedent presents of guilt remov'd,
And wrath transform'd to soothing strains of
   peace ;
Damnation quash'd ; perdition rais'd to life ;
The death-bound heart inspir'd with life anew ;
The dormant functions nerv'd with new-born
   power ;
The tastes, affections, feelings, and delights,
Again attun'd to pure celestial joy,—
Fraught with the precious fruits of Paradise,—
Involves an exercise of pow'r divine,
Till now unknown, amidst Heaven's glorious deeds.

   Hell's horrid groans and imprecations loud
Rebounding from the ever-sinking depths

Of black despair, like echo's dread report
From the deep cav'rns of Vesuvian flame,
In dreadful tones confirm the stern decree,
That guilt must perish in its own misdeeds.
  Yet man surviv'd, a helpless, shrivel'd wreck
Of his primeval glory ; but of hope,
Infus'd within the dreary waste, aware—
Feeble and dim to his uncertain gaze,
Although sufficient to break up the gloom
And hopeless horror of complete despair.
But whence deriv'd ? what its security ?
Or what the pow'r and medium by which
It pierc'd the murky clouds of wrath divine,
And his inherent consciousness of guilt,
With vital warmth to chase despair away ?
Were too mysterious,—less absorbing too,
Than the conviction that it really was ;
Too blind to reason, or to understand,—
Too destitute to cavil, or reject ;
To oracles reveal'd, though dimly couch'd
In parabolic phrase and partial terms,
He earnest listen'd, and sincerely clung
In humble trust. 'Twas faith, and yielded peace ;
For thus he saw in visions, though obscure,
And dispensations suited to his state,
Divine solicitude, compassion, care,—
Sweet indications of restoring grace.
  As time advanc'd, those visions frequent grew,

And more explicit to the humble eye,
Revealing truth significant of good,
Prepar'd in the imperial mind,—bright rays
Of Mercy's hid designs,—of Love unquench'd,
In pity resting on the fallen race,—
That drew the humble eye, with earnest gaze.
To look beyond the heritage of woe,
Into the germs of intercourse with Heaven,
And learn, by earnest study, its import
And consummation in the will Divine,
And find again a refuge in his grace.
Nor was the effort vain.   Benighted hearts,
Lost in the wilds of ignorance and shame,
Beheld the star of Mercy brighter beam,
And shed a radiance on the barren wilds,
That vanquish'd fear, and woo'd the wand'rer
    home ;
Beheld, pervading the Infinite Mind,
Floods of compassion, hitherto unknown,
That outward flow'd, e'en to this distant earth,
Which crush'd rebellion, and constrain'd the heart
To own the influence of their hallow'd sway,
And yield to gratitude, devotion, love ;
To cherish thought refined, and freedom gain,
From the enthralment of apostacy,—
A bright memorial of Almighty grace.
    Those welcome lights from out the mercy seat
Were hail'd with joy by sires of human race,

Whose gladden'd hearts with gratitude beheld
The cheering daybreak bursting into light ;
Diffusing hope, and trust, and heav'nly peace,
Upon their chequer'd pilgrimage below,
And sweet affinity 'twixt earth and heav'n,
That sooth'd their troubles and enhanc'd their
   joys ;
And as they wander'd, upward still they strain'd,
To view its glory in unclouded strength.
Full many a struggling, drooping, wayworn heart,
Has since reviv'd beneath th' effulgent beams,
Whose cloudless splendour rests upon the world :
And in its light preferr'd celestial good,
And virtue's path, that leads to rest above.

CHAPTER VII.

Not mortal ears alone intently heard
Hope's thrilling accents issue from the throne ;
Nor human penetration only knew
Its wond'rous import, certain, though obscure,—
Seraphic hosts attendant heard, and paus'd
In studious amaze, when they beheld,
Outpeering from the secrecy divine,
Perfections hitherto unseen, combin'd,
In union ancient, with those long divulg'd,
Diffusing glory round the great I Am.
More fervent and intense than e'er was seen,
Through previous being in the courts of bliss.
With holy wonder they intently search'd
Bright Mercy's deep designs and hidden ways,

Midst Wisdom's holiest haunts, where she devis'd
Her high achievements of redeeming grace,
Ere man was form'd, or ever angel sung,—
View'd the first feeble ray on Adam shed,
And marvell'd how the wretched sinner liv'd ;
What vital pow'r could penetrate the cold,
Insensate spirit, crush'd by sin and guilt,
And wake within it heaven's exalted praise ;—
Beheld it bright'ning with the lapse of time,
As men increas'd, and in impiety
More hardy grew, by vile confed'racy ;
And farther stray'd, and err'd more grievously,
In groping ignorance of ways divine.

'Twas truth celestial, by contrivance new,
Diffus'd upon the world from heav'nly spheres,
To guide sin's groaning slaves to liberty,—
Increasing ever, as defection spread
Its baleful blight into the human heart,
And prov'd its progress from the source of life ;
For dire experience the sad truth confirm'd,
That human reason, wisdom, and device,
Were totally in vain to guide the soul
Back to the source of its lost happiness,
Or find another equal to its wants.
The humble heart, by such experience taught,
Sought Truth in God, embrac'd the dawning
    light,
And hail'd its increase with exultant joy,

E

As the exponent of heaven's peace and love ;
And in it trusted for true happiness.

There Adam turn'd, and found a refuge safe—
A sweet reversion of his dreadful doom ;
Beheld a something—though obscurely seen—
Illustrative of majesty divine,
That seem'd with compensation richly fraught,
For the dishonour he had on it heap'd,—
Which sooth'd the anguish of his sad remorse,
And drew him back in effort and desire
To humble trust and confidence in Him
Whose hallow'd sway he dar'd to contravert.

There Abel look'd, and in its dawning light
Symbolic shed the Lamb's appeasing blood,
And found acceptance ; in it, too, beheld
Celestial raptures in attendance plac'd
At the unopen'd porch, as yet unpass'd,—
Where mortals now are crowding to their fate ;
To cast the robe of immortality,
By merit not his own, with all its bliss,
Around his spirit, rudely chas'd from time.

There Enoch look'd, and humbly walk'd with
    God ;
And upward rose, above the musty clouds
Of sin and sense, till merging into life,
Surpris'd, he found mortality dissolv'd,
And all its sorrows, like the murky morn
Lost in the glory of meridian day.

There Noah saw, and rear'd his wond'rous
   barque;
That fearless rode upon a shoreless sea,
Above the impious jeers, and godless scorn,
Profanely urg'd to turn his thoughts aside ;
And in the ark not built by human hands
Confiding, found a refuge from his woe.

  There Israel's sire, 'gainst hope, repos'd secure ;
Found peace and favour circling round his path ;
Amidst the stranger, safety ; friendship sweet
In hallow'd converse with a gracious God ;
Beheld what angel vision fail'd to trace
Of heaven's redeeming mercy to mankind,
Through distant generations of the race ;
And in the glory of unclouded truth—
By faith discover'd, and to faith reveal'd,—
Embrac'd the promise that made life his own.

  And Moses, too, and Israel's honour'd seers,
Have seen, and sung, and gloried in its beams ;
And myriads more, unknown, unrecognis'd,—
Save by the eye that penetrates within .
The secrets of all thought,—have in its light
Seen nought but ruin stalking in the train
Of hollow pride, and selfishness, and sin,
Abjured their sway ; submission have renounc'd
Have by its light beheld, and felt the power
Of matchless love, and turn'd again to God ;
And in Him found all elevating good,

For present wants of time, or stor'd secure
In faithful promise for futurity,—
That made them triumph over every foe
That would oppose their ever-onward course,
To the bright joys prepar'd beyond the sky.

   Come, glorious Truth! replete with promise
    sure,
That cheer'd the darkness of primeval night,
Full of triumphant hope and heav'nly peace!
Whose cloudless splendour shines upon my path,
And makes resistance heinous indeed,—
Come, woo my heart to holiness and love,
Which seer, and sire, and saint obscure of old,
By lesser radiance woo'd, saw, and embrac'd;
Infuse therein, as in primeval time,
The living seed, to vegetate and grow,—
Till, 'midst its spreading boughs, each wand'ring
    thought,
Each stray'd affection, faculty, and pow'r,
A refuge finds from agitating fear
In the asylum of redeeming grace.

   Thus did it spread among the human tribes,—
By care celestial watch'd, and water'd oft
By richest streams from Paradise, diffus'd
In type and symbol; gradually reveal'd
To studious eye. Disclos'd to chosen seers
In vision wrapt. Hymn'd in ecstatic song
Of heav'nly minstrelsy, and terms sublime;

In phrase mysterious, or in accents plain,
At public gates of restless human life,
Or silent hour of Nature's still repose,—
To tribes selected for the honour'd charge,
And safe protection of a thing so pure
From hostile insult in an erring world;
Or publish'd loud in hearing of mankind,
To raise their grov'ling thoughts from earth to
    heav'n,—
All as beseem'd to perfect Wisdom meet;
That human wisdom might its folly learn,
And reason feel its impotence to reach,
By light its own, a haven of repose.
Thus revelation, in its varied streams,
Proclaim'd the advent of the promis'd One;
In pregnant symbol, or in statutes clear,
Or strange events, by Providence produc'd,
Fraught with forecasting shadows of the truth,
And rich compassion to the human race.

As race on race swept over Time's brief scene,
And nations rose to momentary pow'r;
Fulfill'd their mission in heaven's high design,
By sov'reign wisdom sway'd, unconscious oft
Of higher impulse than their puny will,
Or holier purpose than their barb'rous schemes
Of rapine, tyranny, and spoil;—yet were
Constrain'd to guard the citadel of Truth;
Its oracles receive, and rally round

Made human crime subservient to His will,
Till time had prov'd all human efforts vain ;
Vain all expedients, all devices vain,
Apart from God ; all else but impotence
To gain for man a shred of happiness.
Then did the clouds of dim dubiety,
Enshrouding type and symbol, disappear ;
And visions oft were seen, and more distinct,
With clearer import to the humble mind ;
Prophetic voice assum'd historic form ;
Predictions ancient into fact emerg'd ;
And Thought, exhausted with her fruitless toil,
Despairing, look'd beyond herself for light ;
In seeming union, nations hush'd their feuds,
Forgot their strife, or in submission bow'd
Beneath the yoke acknowleg'd pow'r inflicts,—
Unconscious quell'd by Heaven's resistless will ;
And sages paus'd, disgusted with their lore,
Crude, dark, and bootless for the heart's repose,
And turn'd instinctive to the sacred courts,
And oracles of truth, to Israel giv'n,—
And studious ponder'd revelations there ;
The world expectant, to the light converg'd,
And hail'd the promise Israel thought its own,
Of old announ'd in halls of heav'nly bliss,
Amidst seraphic wonder, awe, and praise :—
" Behold ! I come, to do thy holy will,
In oracles declar'd, O thou, my God !"

CHAPTER VIII.

In Judah's land, on Bethlehem's fertile plains,
The noiseless flocks luxuriant herbage cropt,
And drank the limpid stream, in silent night ;
When busy man, oblivious of his toil,
'Midst balmy sleep forgot the world's turmoil ;—
The wakeful shepherds, watchful of their charge,
And studious, too, of Israel's dawning hope,
Intent to hail the Star of Jessie rise—
Expected presage of the coming day—
And Shiloh's advent welcome, long foretold,

With glory pregnant to her captive sons ;—
To Sion turn'd, and on the midnight air
Spread hopeful songs of trust.   Invok'd,
In strains devout, the promise long deferr'd,
With meek oblation fervently infus'd
By pious hearts to Sion's holy King ;
In humble faith invok'd the arm divine
To be outstretch'd, as it had been of old,
For Sion's freedom, long in bondage held.

   And as the odour of their incense rose
In sweet perfume, on expectation's wing,
Up to the throne of Israel's cov'nant God,
Loud burst the echo of unnumber'd harps,
By distance mellow'd, on their wond'ring ear.
Those strains sublime, as nearer they approach'd,
Melodious swell'd in rapture more intense,
Fraught with salvation.   The celestial peal
Awoke astonishment, and deep amaze,
And trembling fear, within the shepherds' breasts ;
While glowing accents fill'd their humble ear,
In heav'nly cadence cloth'd, replete with love :—
" To you at length the promise is fulfill'd !
The Child foretold now dwells upon the earth ;—
Heaven's highest, noblest gift—the Son belov'd ;
His name the Wonderful, the Counsellor ;
Beyond all wisdom and above all power ;
The Father everlasting, the Prince of Peace ;—
Whose glorious kingdom shall endure for aye,

Supreme, benignant, through all coming time,
O'er ev'ry clime, and kindred, tongue, and tribe,
With glory pregnant to God's mighty name ;
Peace to the world, and goodwill to mankind."
   Thus sang seraphic hosts, while o'er the plains
Heaven's radiance brightly shone. Night drew
   aside ;
And joy, exultant in celestial smiles;
Brought reassurance to the shepherds' hearts,
Alarm'd by conscious guilt, when brought so near
Those glorious heralds of the great Supreme ;
Their fears dispell'd by those ecstatic strains,
Whose gracious import fill'd their minds with
   peace.
With hearts inspir'd by gratitude and hope,
And joyous faith upon the promise stay'd,
They bent their steps to Judah's regal seat,
In glorious days of David's pious sway ;
And there amaz'd, by promise realis'd,
They found Messiah : Heaven's appointed One—
So long foretold, and now at length bestow'd.
   Nor did they seek alone. Minds more acute ;
Of higher tone ; to cultivation prone ;
And deeply vers'd in Nature's course abstruse ;
From eastern climes, where early day reveals
Her golden treasures, to awake delight ;
In contemplation on celestial themes
Most studious bent ; meanwhile to gross pursuits

Of sense averse,—unworthy of their choice ;
Prone to discover more etherial joys ;—
With vision upward turn'd in earnest gaze,
To scan the glories of the upper spheres ;
Which gild the lofty canopy of earth,
Their revolutions mark, or their increase,
As from the vista of infinite space
Some distant orb is heralded to view ;
If thus, perchance amidst the blazing throng,
A glimpse is caught of the almighty hand
That trims their lights, and paints their varied hues,
And guides their courses with unerring care.

Thus studious they,—when, lo ! a meteor new,
And strangely vivid with unwonted hues,
In sudden lustre broke upon their view,—
By special law, for special end design'd,
It points significant, and leads the way
Of penetration, to the humble scene
Of Heaven and Earth's solicitude, where lay
The Virgin Mother with her Child Divine.

In wond'ring awe, the wise and simple met
To gaze astonish'd on one common sight ;
Each, with the grasp of his respective strength,
Concentrate on one view, in deep amaze ;
Debarr'd was earthly pomp and human pride—
Unfit attendants on the hallow'd scene ;
Too rude and gross to witness the descent
Of highest glory to the humblest depth ;

No steel-clad legions fill'd the outer halls,
Nor loyal crowds assembled in the courts
Of splendid palace, courteously resign'd,
In humble tribute to the Lord of all ;
No soft refinements, in luxuriance spread
Around the portals of mortality,
To soothe the anguish, tributary laid
On ev'ry entrant, to earth's sterile scenes ;
No downy couch, exuberant of wealth ;
No aid obsequious in the trying hour ;
No deputies of earth, accredited
By high authority, to certify,
And herald forth to all her potentates—
Too mean for vassalage—his high approach ;
No studied phrase, and blandishment of speech,
From oily tongue of insincerity,
And heart repugnant to the utterance,
His advent hail'd among the sons of men ;
These filthy steps ambition meanly climbs
To reach the giddy heights of human sway ;
But there ! no pomp nor pageantry are seen
To strike the eye and wake ambition's flame.
And so earth's sons, cold, calculating souls,
Withheld their greetings, sympathy, regard ;
Withheld their welcome, and refus'd to own
His dignity and worth, who seem'd to sense
A wither'd root, sprung from the parched ground
Devoid of form, attraction, comeliness,

To please the eye of sense, and only fit
To be rejected as a worthless thing.
And yet essential glory lay conceal'd
Upon that humble couch, in meanest form,
Hid in a human frame, 'midst cold neglect,
And earth's debasement, weakness, and disdain,
Impervious to the view of carnal eye.
By entrance new,—apart from Nature's rule,
Free from pollution's taint,—the Holy One
Stoop'd down to sojourn among mortal scenes :
The base arena, where His mighty deeds
Of love and mercy should completion meet.

  Mere human reason, erring and corrupt,
Though deep her int'rest in His enterprise,
Must stand aside from the mysterious scene,—
Too weak to grasp transactions so sublime ;
Involv'd too deeply in the mournful cause
To be admitted to the hallow'd spot.
Ungift'd oxen girt in instinct's bands,—
The humble produce of creative power,
Of reason void, and therefore less involv'd
In impious guilt,—seem'd more appropriate
To witness scenes so pure ; their stalls less
  vile,—
A manger less repugnant for a couch
  herein to cradle Purity itself ;
And there, amidst bleak poverty's chill blast—
Humiliation crushing as the grave—

The Prince of Glory lay, a helpless child,
In meek submission to the will divine.
 Adoring shepherds knelt in awe profound ;
Sages, astonish'd, bow'd in deep amaze ;
A holier awe fill'd the capacious mind
Of hosts seraphic, whose expanded grasp
Embrac'd a wider range of its import ;
Struck mute with wonder, nearer they approach'd,
To view the combination of Almighty power,—
'Mong wonders still so wonderful and strange,—
Where the perfections of divinity
Were all display'd, in glory more sublime ;
In boundless power, and wisdom more acute,—
Resource more various,—love more full and free,
Than in the dawn of time, when by the fiat
Of energy supreme, a universe
Emerg'd, from womb of nothing, into life.
 The dark enigma of four thousand years :—
" Who can from impure, purity produce ?
Or clean, from unclean bring ?"—solution found
In Beth'lem's lowly stalls.   Antagonism join'd.
Divinity unseen, in union bound
By bond perpetual and intimate,
Yet still unblended with that mortal frame.
In that weak infant, hush'd on virgin breast,
So lovely in its utter helplessness,—
That wakes spontaneous sympathy and love ;
Unlike a thing of earth, and, oh ! unlike

Its high original ; by men renounc'd,
As fit associate for the bestial tribes ;
Whose first deep wail of helplessness was sooth'd
By kindred weakness of maternal love ;
Its wants and griefs anticipated there.
In it, conceal'd upon a human breast
Obscure, in depths of poverty and gloom,
Was peerless Majesty,—and all His own.
All contrast met in Him.   Glory supreme
Met and conjoin'd with insignificance ;
Neglect with honour ; weakness with all power ;
The fullness of eternity embrac'd
Time's utmost need ; the feeble dawn of life
To all duration intimately bound ;
Supreme dominion—universal sway ;
Unquestion'd glory there repos'd.   There, too,
Unfeign'd submission, with the neck bent down
Beneath the galling yoke, to lift the load
And bear the anguish of imputed wrath ;
All merit own'd all guilt ; and holiness
Consummate misery embrac'd ; grief hugg'd
Tranquillity ; unerring rectitude
Receiv'd the sinner's brand, and bore his shame ;
Among the vile the vilest was esteem'd.
All met in him.   It was the cent'ral point,
Whence all extremes diverg'd, and back return'd
For clear solution in his wond'rous life.
And o'er that clouded brow, mature in woe,

What mercy hover'd ! what benevolence
And melting pity for degen'rate man !
What high regard for rectitude divine !
For Heaven's bright honour, impiously assail'd !
What firm decision, by atonement made
In substitution for earth's guilty race,
To reconcile, and blend them both in one,
Was hidden there within that infant frame !

   And, oh ! to know that deep mysterious love ;
Its magnitude and pow'r to comprehend ;
That robed it all in holiness divine,
And shed a glory o'er the wond'rous One,
(Though inapparent to the carnal eye,)
Too bright and pure for high seraphic gaze.
Oh, what compassion ! matchless mercy this !
That drew the Son, eternally belov'd,
From hidden glory of infinite bliss ;
From oneness true, entire, through being passed
Back in the bosom of eternity,
With Godhead unexplor'd, in essence pure ;
From adoration, worship, ceaseless praise,
By countless myriads of seraphic hosts,
Forever swelling through the realms of bliss,
In universal plaudits to his name ;
And boundless glory, and unutter'd praise,
With richer flow, in more ecstatic strains,
Increasing ever as existence rolls ;—
Drew him from all, to be enwrapt in shame,

F

And wear the garb of vile humanity,
And bear the curse humanity had earn'd.

How comprehend a wonder so sublime?
Men fix dimensions to the rolling spheres;
They cast the line of measurement across
The mighty space that distances this earth
From yon bright speck that glimmers into view;
From orb to orb, from sphere to sphere, they leap,
And tell the true proximity of each.
Give that a name, locality, amount!
Too vast and varied for the human thought
To comprehend.   Still the expanse is known,
And yields to calculation's mighty grasp;
Thence penetrate into the wilds unseen—
Discovers being in untrodden space,
Affixes distance, number, orbit, speed,
Proximity to all.   Their magnitude
And revolutions calculate, and tell,
Which, when reveal'd, remain a myst'ry still;
And yet, when told, how meagre is the sum
Compar'd with the vast residue unknown?

Angelic thought capacious sweeps afar,
Beyond the range of amplest human grasp;
Computes extent, embraces magnitude,
In regions of immeasurable space,
Where human thought can never penetrate;
But limit still is there.   Domains exist,
By Seraph eye and scrutiny unseen,

Whose ample glories blaze, beyond the pale
Of recognition, by those potent minds.
  Archangel vision even there may float
In tranquil study, wonder, and delight ;
Soar out to distance, till it seems absorb'd
In chaos undefin'd ; there bound'ry fix ;
Limit and form apparent to his view ;
Conceive, embrace, and clearly comprehend,
With nice precision, all the vast domain ;
Bring in the ample survey, and confine
The glorious whole within a finite thought.
But 'tis his own.   The boundless view remains
In all its amplitude with him alone ;
None less exalted could the circuit make
Of magnitude so great ; yet 'tis embrac'd,
And yields its greatness to created mind.
  In things minute, amidst the viewless clefts
Of tiny nothingness, beneath the glance
Of recognition, man can penetrate,—
By art assisted, in acute research,—
And there discover tokens of design,
Formation, adaptation, symmetry,
The powers and functions of instinctive life,
With its diversified activities,—
To unseen atoms, sentient being give ;
Divide, and sub-divide, their sep'rate parts,
Ascribing place and faculties, distinct,
In operation for a noble end,

Until perception fails to recognise,
And owns a depth in the invisible,
Which human penetration cannot reach.

  Angelic vision, balanc'd more acute,
With keener glance and nicer pow'rs endow'd,
Beholds a teeming world, beneath the range
Of human eye, by highest art sustain'd;
Discovers adaptation and design,
And function perfect, in its whole detail,
Within the sacred innermost recess
Of dim intangibility. With ease
Explores the hidden depths, unveils to thought
The viewless atom, dang'ling on the verge
Of nought, where the material seems absorb'd,
And into spirit merg'd,—for that claims form,
And local space, and functions perfect too,
And calls it matter still. Beneath it all
Existence still resides, by wisdom form'd
In undiminish'd strength, which only He
Who gave it being can perceive and know;
Yet He who gave to magnitude its space,
And to minute precision, may invest
Intelligence with powers for the survey,
And admiration of the glorious whole.
But in this love, that mov'd the Son belov'd
To hide his glory in the manger couch,
Dimensions are unknown. Reason admits
Its impotence to scan; Intelligence

Retreats to shades of mute astonishment,
And humbly craves permission to adore.
Itself, its own criterion, defies
All exposition or comparison.
  Oh, for some bright conceptions of the deed !
Crumbs from the Master's table,—to inspire
A deeper glow of gratitude and praise,
For such stupendous love, from whence He came.
Source of all being ! Living font of Life !
Sum of all parts, and centre of the whole !
On whose right arm creation rests secure,
And round His being ever onward moves,
In tracts as varied as its countless hosts ;
And ever bright'ning in perfection's hues,
As being is prolong'd and access gain'd,
To nearer precincts of the great Supreme,
Who fires the spirits which surround the throne
With holiest zeal, and fires them every one,
And tunes their harps with everlasting praise,
Inspires ten thousand times ten thousand hearts
To hymn that praise in one ecstatic song,
Of loud acclaim to his Almighty name,—
The just recipient and theme of all,—
He from the glory of essential bliss,
And unapproach'd tranquillity, serene
In condecension, stooping to receive
The tribute due to His imperial throne.
  That He, constrain'd by love so marvellous,

Should own its sway, so to its dictates yield,
So wrap His being in its tender folds,
That, notwithstanding sin's repugnancy,—
Nay, for that very cause, should join Himself
To vile, degraded, base, apostate man,
In union absolute, compress'd within
The fragile frame-work of humanity ;—
So far exceeds the range of finite thought
That reason fails to grasp the glorious truth,
And in adoring gratitude delights
To own its weakness and survey the fruits.

CHAPTER IX.

So stoop'd the Son Divine.   He must be man.
None else could enter man's experience,
Or sound the depths of his degraded state,
Or know his trials, and with them sympathise ;
None else but man could take the sinner's place,
To bear his burden and perform his task,
As justice claim'd that he himself should do.
    A creature !   That were marvellous indeed !
Though in a seraph's glory richly clad,
With all the splendour finitude could bear,
Apart from aught involving charge of guilt.

He bow'd, a servant to the law divine ;
A creature's duty and obedience gave,
As obligation righteously demands
From the recipient of all-gracious gifts,
On man conferr'd with an unsparing hand ;
Himself supreme, yet He submission yields—
A perfect service, equal to the sum
Of all divergence by the human race ;
Makes good what they withheld ; yields just return
And restitution for their base misdeeds.

For whose misdeeds ?   Does limit circumscribe
The rich provisions of infinite grace !
And modify obedience, or curtail
The dread intensity of woe endur'd,
In just proportion to the number sav'd ?
Or, unrestrain'd by high electing love,
Is it a price for ev'ry ruin'd one,
That when ignor'd involves a fruitless waste
Of deepest anguish on the victim laid ?

What's that to thee, O sinner ?   Does it change
Thy duty, or responsibility ?
Or what to thee, O minister of Christ ?
Dar'st thou conceal His love " *among the stuff*,"
Or make a stinted offer of His grace ?

Yon stranded ship, dash'd by the furious storm,
Is breaking up, amidst the angry waves ;
Her crew, benumb'd and helpless, perish must,
Unless assistance snatch them from their fate.

Oh! if that lifeboat, urged into the deep,
Could pass the jutting reef; resist the tide;
Surmount the tempest; all may yet escape!
See, it is done! she gains the fated ship,
And one by one receives the famish'd crew,
Save one. He will not. Reason is dethron'd.
He madly rushes to a dangling spar,
And leaps exulting on a crested wave,
And, with a cheer, sinks in the briny deep.
Was *he* excluded in the means prepar'd?
Nay, not the number, but the danger seen;
The question was—how reach the ship at all?
    'Tis not the *number* of sin-ruin'd souls
That fill'd the cup of the Redeemer's woe
With taste so bitter. Numbers *limit* prove.
It was to reach the hell-deserving guilt,
And in their stead its consequence endure;
To rescue one, the least defil'd of men,
From the disasters of his dreadful fate;
The Mighty One must occupy his place,
Exhaust the utmost of his dire deserts,
Extending o'er duration's endless range,—
Make restitution for that period lost,
In meet devotion to the great Supreme.
He who is equal to the mighty task
Does that for one,—that equal is for all,
And myriads of apostate worlds besides.
    'Twas restitution to the Law divine,

For disobedience grievously maintain'd ;
Complete devotion, fruit of perfect love,
Felt, and express'd, in ev'ry word and deed,
To the Imperial will,—an image bright,
In humble miniature of lowly life,
Of attributes divine.   Unswerving truth,
And holiness sustain'd, and fervent love,
Confiding trust for ever bursting forth,
On ev'ry side, from an o'erflowing heart,
Maintain'd throughout against the bold intrigue
And luring wiles of Satan's matchless skill,
In opposition urg'd by rude assault,
Insinuations vile, or tortuous doubt ;
In single conflict, pregnant with deceit,
As when at first man yielded to his sway,
Or by his agents, clad in human form,
With quenchless ardour aiming at his fall.
  'Twas restitution too, to human kind,
For selfishness indulg'd, unfeeling pride,
And disregard—each of his Brother's weal ;
His touch was health ; His word of power was life ;
His presence comfort to the bleeding heart ;
His tears were all for them ; His counsels too ;
For them His toils, and weariness, and woes ;
His gracious hand shower'd blessings everywhere ;
On friend or foe alike ; His loving heart
And hand were ever pouring good ;
Unmoved by slander, unrepress'd by hate,

By opposition undeterr'd, unchill'd
By base ingratitude ;—evil for good
Was His requittal for unceasing love.
  'Twas new to earth. Its cold unfeeling sod
Ne'er felt the tread of goodness so sublime ;
Ne'er saw benevolence so rich and pure ;
Or so diffus'd, and exercis'd
With patience so exhaustless and refin'd ;
So universal, constant, and sincere ;
Full of celestial fragrance, drawing down
Heaven's blessed sunshine to refresh the world,—
Repeated day by day throughout his life
With dignity sublime, unaw'd by power
Puff'd into frowning pride ; and unabash'd
By crushing poverty ; applause or blame,
Ingratitude or love, in vain assail'd
Or modified His pure benevolence.
Those mighty umpires of all human things,
Which guide the thoughts and doings of mankind,
Fail'd to control one action of His life ;
Serene and tranquil, as the slumb'ring lake
On whose still bosom not a zephyr plays,
He met Time's impious scorn, dislike, reproach,—
Gave Heavenly kindness for a foe's return,—
The tear of pity for relentless hate,—
Best deeds for worst,—the sweet for bitter gave,—
As God alone can give ; while through the gloom
Of His eventful life, dense as a cloud

Oppression, wrong, injustice, cruelty,
By man inflicted on his brother man !
To live therein and breathe its putrid air,
Become its victim, bearing the full weight
Of its malignity, and yet survive !
Love seeks return,—that is its very life,—
A heart responsive to receive its beams,
And glow with gratitude beneath.
Repuls'd, malign'd, its richest deeds defam'd,
What must it suffer in this ruthless world ?

  Alas ! we have no gauge to sound the depth
Of crushing pain His servitude involv'd,
That trac'd deep lines of sorrow on His brow,
And wrung his heart with misery and grief.

  Let souls awaken'd to an inward taste
For what is pure, celestial, and refin'd,—
Attun'd to throb with piety and love,—
To honour God and magnify His name,—
Say what distress impiety conveys ;
What wounds unfeeling selfishness inflicts,
Upon the heart when soften'd and subdu'd,
By but a spark of the exalted flame,
That fill'd the bosom of the Holy One ;
And thence conceive, as erring ignorance
May apprehend of all pervading worth,
What He, who sees, in high seraphic throngs
And Heavenly spheres, dim spots of vanity,
Must undergo in this accursed world.

Oh, where, in all His weary, troubled life,
Was there a sunny spot of peace and joy
Whereon to rest His lacerated heart,
And gain fresh courage for approaching woe !
Not in His infancy,—cast on the care
Of earth's most abject ones ; consign'd to trust
To other's bounty, for a safe escape
From cruelty in regal power enthron'd,
Striving, by impious lawlessness and crime,
To crush His life and frustrate all His love.
Not in His youth,—associate with vice
Rank to a proverb ; 'midst abounding crime ;
His Heavenly worth and youthful zeal repress'd
By meek submission, poverty, and toil.
Not in His riper years,—whose every hour
Came deeper laden with appointed grief,
And every step involv'd in deeper shame.

     Yet from the Manger,—where astonish'd hosts
Beheld their Lord weep on a Mother's breast,
And wail a mortal cry,—on to the Cross
Of agony and shame, where he expired ;
Meek resignation to the will divine,
Compassion for the misery of man,
Untiring patience and benevolence,
Shone forth conspicuous in His holy life,
With prescient eye, exulting in the fruit
Of His sore travail ; His forecasting love,
Resting in secret joy on ransom'd souls,

                                             G

Inspired anew with energy divine ;
With motives hitherto unknown ; and strains,
'Till now unheard within the realms of bliss,
In ceaseless praises to the Triune God.
He trode, unfalt'ring, sorrow's thorny way,—
In strict obedience to all righteous claims,
In substitution for His erring ones,—
Unaided, and alone, against all powers
And machinations vile of earth and hell,
That clos'd more densely on His onward way
As He drew nearer to the fatal goal.

   Calm and resign'd he held the dreadful cup,
And knew its contents, to the bitter dregs,
(Foreknowledge ! what addition to His woe !)
All its ingredients ever in His view,
Its dismal terrors, ever in His soul,
Corroding deeper as their sum increas'd ;
While strong desire, anticipating all
With dread forecasting, striving to outrun
Time's tardy progress, seems to overleap
The intervening ills, to feel the worst.
As restless man, oft would the future grasp,
And chide events which linger in his way,
Is fain to reach, by some less lengthy route,
The goal of hope, whereon his heart is set,—
So press'd His anxious soul to reach the sum
Of anguish understood, and justly view'd
In all its horrid magnitude and woe :

To reach the point, where issues marvellous—
In conflict sore, not doubtfully are hung—
Shall be disclos'd, and suffering withdrawn ;
Where Prophets meet, and symbols are explain'd,
And types fulfill'd, and shadows are dispell'd ;
Where Time's permitted deeds, to truth oppos'd,
Are harmoniz'd with Wisdom's high design
And hidden ways, in secret ruling all ;
Results educing, never entertain'd
By their enactors—directing their fit place
And proper influence in the great designs
Of mercy to the world.   Where sin appears
In all its naked filthiness and shame,
In hideous contrast to eternal truth ;
Apostacy attempting the last throw
For vile supremacy ; Ingratitude
With shame grown fierce ; Impiety full bent
To hide its monstrous nature in the blood
Of all perfection.

   To reach the point, when hell's malignant
      hate
Is gather'd up like strength of mighty man ;
Its legions marshall'd, all its arts conven'd,
For struggle worthy of its vast renown,
And for a stake full worthy of its pride ;
The point when men, exceeding all the race
In slavish bondage and servility
To hell's accursed sway each for himself,

In monstrous blindness to his fate therein,
Cast in his willing aid (how keen it stung !)
To swell the force of Tophet's horrid storm.

    The point, when wrath gush'd, like a mighty
      flood,
From secret place of holiness divine,
Assailing Him with overwhelming sense
Of all demerit and abandonment ;
Left to the prowess of His own right hand,—
Beneath the sin of an apostate race,—
To grapple with all evil, and maintain
By light inherent His integrity.

    Reflect, my soul ! Could less than God do
      this ?
Could you rely on finitude to bear
Your single soul across the fiery deep,
And place it safe in Heaven ? If not, who then
Beneath the Throne of the Eternal, may
Provide redemption for a fallen race ?

    As He drew near the altar's rising pile,
And felt the fervour of its kindling flame,
The prospect dismal and appalling grew,
And Nature quailing with astonishment
And consternation sore, in wailing plaint
Reliev'd the burden of its dread dismay :
" My soul in anguish sinks ; what shall I say ?
Claim as a proof of undiminish'd love,
Subsisting still within a Father's breast,

A truce to woe? exemption from this hour?
Nay! for this hour I own the human name;
Its dread dismay I would not now escape,
So fraught with glory to the Triune God;
Be that secur'd, where it has been withheld,
I swerve not from the travail of My soul."

CHAPTER X.

———

'TWAS in a garden, 'midst the sunny bowers
Of innocence, and peace, and ample joy,
And ever fresh delight, that Adam fail'd
In his obedience—lost primeval bliss ;
Stranger to want ; no good from him withheld ;
Provision ample to maintain his post ;
Motive and strength in measure full bestowed,—
Full as the finite could infinite grasp,—
Yet thus enrich'd, he swerv'd, and was undone.
In such a place his Substitute must meet
The dire infliction of sin's just awards,
And bear the anguish of its heinous guilt.
The spirit fails, imagination faints

To sum the dreadful magnitude of woe
That gather'd round Him in that fatal hour.
Night hung her mantle o'er the busy world,
And, like a fun'ral pall, envelop'd earth;
No glim'ring star betoken'd being else;
No breath was felt, to stir the stagnant air;
No sound reveal'd life's presence to His sense;
From zephyr, rill, or shrub, or living thing,
Sense seem'd withdrawn; Nature was paralyz'd;
While he in loneliness entire,—alone
In the vast universe, dark as the grave,—
Cross'd Kedron's brook, into the dismal shade
Of silence insupportable.

    The bonds were loos'd that had forever knit
The Mighty God to His co-equal Son;
Love,—glorious in its streams, but in its font
And essence, how sublime!—ignor'd Him now,
And all its manifold delights withdrew
In retributive ire.   The interchange
Of mutual oneness and complacency,
That flow'd perpetual through the dateless roll
Of previous being's vast infinitude,
In deep ineffable tranquillity,
Asunder reft by force of wrath divine,
To secret haunts of holiness retir'd.
Oh, 'twas impenetrable solitude,
Dark, deep desertion, and abandonment,
By Heaven's great Sire in wrath vindictive clad,

No sense of mutual bliss was left him now,
Nor conscious token of Divine regard,
To ease the horror of His dread astonishment.
Forsaken thus, demerit dire assail'd,
And urg'd her terrors in His holy mind ;
All guilt of every hue, kind, or degree,
By man contracted, centred upon Him ;
Each thought, word, deed divergent (all were so),
Its aggravation and atrocity,
Crush'd in upon His soul with its full tale
Of woe ineffable.   Amazing thought !
That human soul could bear the dreadful sum.

    Thus crush'd was he by essence of despair,—
'Neath which existence quiver'd in dismay,—
Hell, prompt and watchful for the weakest point,
Seiz'd the dread hour with stern malignity ;
Urg'd the transcendant magnitude of guilt,—
Its hideous stains as not to be effac'd,
But deep'ning ever in the victim's heart ;
All vile suggestions, hideous to the mind,
At variance with fidelity to heav'n,
Were urg'd with ardour and persistency,
As only fiends can urge ; distrust, and doubt,
That the infliction of Jehovah's wrath
Was aim'd at him, not at the sin he bore ;
And that perdition hung upon the stroke,
Inflicting anguish more intense, than due
To the extent of man's apostacy ;

That the exactions Justice claim'd as right,
Were strain'd beyond benignity and love ;
That pow'r existed, had the will been there,
To gain the end by less repulsive means ;
That human nature, though inspir'd and stay'd
By true divinity, was all too weak,
Untested as it was, for such a load ;
Rashly conceiv'd that failure must ensue :
Hence timeous flight was wisdom's prudent course,
To save the honour of Jehovah's name ;
Besides, the prize, unworthy of the price,
Should be relinquish'd, and the pain eschew'd ;
For such austerity on part of God
Is ample proof of love forever gone.

Temptations vile, by artifice conceal'd,
'Increas'd the darkness of his troubl'd soul,
And ting'd his horror with a deadlier hue.
Sin, hideous and disgusting, rush'd in floods
Through ev'ry sense and feeling of his heart,
And closer press'd upon his vivid view,
To lodge its poison, and the soul subvert ;
Conviction dreadful flash'd, and fearfulness,
In consternation and amazement sore
Woke apprehension terrible to bear ;—
Dried up the conscious sustenance of life,
And shut him in to his unaided strength,—
To the supplies essentially his own.
Within, the terrors of incipient death

Spread desolation over ev'ry thought ;
Beclouded reason ; rectitude bedim'd ;
Obscur'd perception of eternal truth,
And apprehension of unfailing love ;
With all the glory to be realis'd
From his endurance, agony, and shame,
Not hung in doubtful balance on his arm ;
Deep call'd to deep, and wrath urg'd billows,
      dash'd
With fearful fury on His holy head,—
Sensation shudder'd, while demerit rose
To vast dimensions in the gloom profound ;
And hate and scorn exerted all their might
And art to overwhelm Him with despair.

  He stood alone ! left to essential might ;
A rock of ages, 'midst a sea of wrath—
A shoreless ocean into fury toss'd ;
Abandon'd by all good, save what arose
From the resources in Himself contain'd,
He bore the malice hell had cherished long,
Against the spoiler of its hated sway ;
No friendly voice of sympathy was heard
To break His terror or assuage His grief ;
No clefts of refuge were to Him disclos'd
Within the secrets of a Father's love :
His refuge in Himself ; His succour there,—
The human in divine ; by it sustain'd,
He stood invincible.   Justice enforc'd

Her plea, unwavering and unmitigate ;
With stern integrity preferr'd her claims
To restitution to th' imperial throne ;
And on Him laid the appalling load of guilt,
'Neath which alone, as mortals cannot be,
Devoid of aught His anguish to relieve,
He trode the winepress of infinite ire ;
Endur'd the fierceness of devouring flame,
And drank the cup of dread astonishment ;
While from eternal rectitude and truth
The stern behest rung like a peal of doom :—
" Awake ! O sword ! against my great compeer !
Relentless pierce into His holy heart,
Who is my Chosen, and my Well-belov'd !
No tender yearnings may avert the stroke,
Or mitigate the anguish it inflicts ;
Gird on thy strength ; let Justice state her claims—
Each jot and tittle of her high demands
In full draw up ; its injuries recount ;
Collect its catalogue of rights withheld ;
All disobedience, insult, and foul scorn—
All opposition, and dislike, sum up ;
Its aggravation, issues, and results,
As by omniscience seen, array'd against
My chosen ones,—and to their Substitute
Transfer the vast amount. Let Vengeance rise,
With glowing wrath and retribution arm'd ;
Unchain her secret woes, long pent within

The records of the past, or reaching forth
Into the future of the world's misdeeds,—
And let it all in fulness on Him fall."

Oh ! what transactions press'd into that hour
Of deepest darkness ! seen alone by Him
Who from behind the murky clouds of wrath
Beheld all things ; and by hell's wily king,
Begirt with all his potency and art,
To gain the conflict, and the Son subdue.
What mystery was there !   God pledg'd for man-!
Beneath his sin and guilt—beneath its doom—
To take his place amidst perdition's flames,
And by His blood to quench its horrid woes !
Man pledg'd for God !   To vindicate His law ;
Maintain its high authority ; enforce
The stainless honour of the will divine ;
And testify before the universe
His indignation at iniquity,
Wherever seen ; and show its certain fruits ;
To prove His matchless love and pity strong ;
The earnest yearnings of His holy mind
For the infusion of His Spirit's grace ;
His strong aversion to man's utter woe ;
And fond desire that he should turn—and live.

Man may not pry into the secret grief
Of the great Daysman, with His hand on both,
And Nature wond'rous to them both allied,
And both sustaining in His conflict sore ;

While consternation and astonishment,
And terrible dismay and anguish keen,
Pour'd all their floods o'er His abandon'd soul ;—
Yet still He clung, amidst their torrents fierce,
To ancient terms of Heaven's supreme regard,
And bow'd submissive to Jehovah's will ;
And stood, because he clung invincible,
Till resignation sooth'd His quaking soul,
Evinc'd by Faith's unshaken utterance :—
" My God ! My God ! why hast Thou Me cast
    off ?
Oh ! why art Thou so far from helping Me,
And from the hearing of My grievous plaint ?
In water deep, in miry clay I sink,
Wherein no standing is.   The pains of hell,
With all Thy terrors strange, encompass Me.
Men shoot the lip in scorn, and shake the head,
And triumph o'er the troubles of My soul.
Like water I'm pour'd out ; My strength departs ;
Wy heart is melted ; I draw nigh to death ;—
Haste to deliver ; there is none to help ;
Be not far off—for death is very near,
And all Thy billows have Me overflown ;
Let Me not sink ; deliver from the pit.
Why should Thy terrors swallow Me outright,
Or hell's despair inclose Me in its bars ?
Its arrows deeply in My bosom pierce.
But Thou art holy, Thou that ever dwell'st

Among the praises Israel Thee accords :
In Thee their trust was never put to shame,—
For when they trusted Thou deliverance brought'st.
If this cup may not pass till all is drunk,
Thy will, not Mine, O Father ! I obey."

It was the hour of hell's supremacy,
When dubious hope upon the balance hung ;
When one false step,—a slight divergent thought,
Infus'd impatience, doubt, or discontent,—
Would bring disaster on His glorious work,
And shroud His name in weakness and disgrace.

Wrath from Infinitude full well was known,
Restrain'd alone by creature strength to bear ;
But wrath infinite cannot be conceiv'd,—
Ev'n hell's experience knows not the amount,—
Yet there it presses on that stricken One !
All might against all might is equal poise ;
Infinite wrath laid on infinite strength
May be indur'd, but, in addition, press
Satanic hate and man's ingratitude—
Reason concludes—the issue must be plain.

So malice judg'd, while Justice was endur'd,
By instant refuge in the secret place
Of his own Godhead ; and in triune bond,
Seal'd and confirm'd by the eternal mind,
And grasp'd unwav'ring in the hour of need ;
Thus Faith triumphant, with her moorings fix'd
Within the veil, outrode the mighty storm.

CHAPTER XI.

GREAT deeds betoken might, excite applause,—
Exalt to admiration and renown ;
The more endur'd, the more invincible
Appears the suff'rer ; when heroic borne,
'Tis true sublimity, which few can reach.
There, 'midst the depths of His unutter'd woe,
The great Redeemer like a pillar stood,—
To Heav'n more precious, and more fear'd by hell.
 Yet all was not endur'd in shades of night.
No ; 'twas the rule of that mysterious life,
From manger to the grave ; extremes combin'd,
And doubl'd ev'ry pang. Nor fail'd it here ;
His secret haunts, to perfidy well known,

By it disclos'd to hireling ruffian bands,—
Befitting instruments of demon hate,
And crime more odious than ev'n hell could
  match ;—
Dragg'd through the mire of mockery and shame,
Indignity, and scorn, in open day ;
To sacrilegious, mask'd hypocrisy,
And venal judgment, and vile perjury ;
Branded with infamy ; like felon scourg'd ;
Contemn'd, rejected as a worthless thing ;
Reproach'd, derided by the very race
On whose behalf His suff'rings were endur'd.

  Oh, vile ingratitude ! what in the cup
Of bitterness can penetrate so deep,—
So agonize and pain the holy One,
Keen in proportion as the gift is great,
Or the inducements to confer it small ?
For man He suffers, and from him receives
The deepest pang that baseness can inflict.
It seems as if perfection were too weak,
And love too fragile for the fatal shock.

  Grim fiends exultant triumph'd in the scene,
Outvieing Tophet's blasphemy and rage ;
By agency so fit, or by themselves,
They eager press'd considerations vile,
In varied form, by artifice disguis'd,
Upon His clouded view.   Desertion urg'd
With keener ardour to instill despair—

Denied His dignity and worth ; contemn'd
His high relation, now by shame obscur'd ;
Assum'd a higher grade ; own'd lesser guilt,
And suff'ring less degrading and intense ;
Endurance less, for less depravity,—
Therefore the victims of a milder fate ;
And in derision held His woe, like theirs,
Was the result of Heaven's abandonment ;
And His rejection to the puny rage
Of man,—the vassals of satanic sway,—
Involv'd his vassalage, and fealty due,
To man's hereditary potentate,
If thus, perchance, amidst the pangs of shame,
The Holy One might for an instant quit
His hold of life, or fail to recognise
His high position in the court of heav'n ;
And so admit aught less than purity
Within the region of His holy mind.
The shame increas'd, and horror grew more dense,
As step by step He pass'd the impious courts,
To sanctity ordain'd ; the judgment hall ;
The Holy City, delug'd with her crimes ;
His sentence heard, and His denial, too ;
The prickly crown, the lacerating scourge,—
The ignominious robe, the insult, too ;
And reach'd the climax of unequall'd woe
On Calv'ry's Cross—a spectacle of shame.
    Angels, appall'd, drew nearer to the throne,

H

For greater safety from the horrid scene ;
All agencies, above, below, seem'd loose
From their allegiance to Jehovah's throne ;
And in grasp of hell's infernal king.

Nature appear'd on dissolution's verge,
As if the hand that built her compact frame,
And knit her spheres, had suddenly relax'd,
And grown too feeble to sustain the care
And pond'rous burden of her varied tribes ;
Day hung its head, and prematurely fled,
Asham'd to witness wickedness so great ;
Night threw her mantle, like a robe of shame,
To hide the frantic doings of mankind ;
Earth's iron bands gave way ; her secret depths
Convulsively upheav'd, and bellow'd forth,
In groans and agitation's travail sore,
And trembl'd 'neath impiety so foul ;
Creation quiver'd in the throes of death.
Yet men, besotted with insensate hate,
Rush'd madly on to consummate their crimes ;
All heedless though the fabric of the earth
Seem'd giving way beneath their guilty tread,
Recoiling from atrocity so base.

Death paus'd, astonish'd at his own success,
And stagger'd at his bold temerity.
In ghastly desperation, he resolv'd
To stake his gloomy empire and renown
Upon the issue ; and suspicious quit

His grasp upon the grave ; to summon strength
That never yet had fail'd ; and brace the nerve
That ne'er had shrunk, in weakness or disgust,
Amidst the carnage of four thousand years ;—
To meet and grapple with the Prince of Life.

The Grave, oblivious of its ancient charge,
And ravenous for more illustrious prey,
Impatient grew ; less studious to retain
The countless throng on which it long had gorg'd ;
Who rous'd, stalk'd forth to see what monstrous
    deeds
Disturb'd the slumbers of their long repose,
And them report to horrify the tomb.

Not all the arrows of infinite wrath,—
The utmost guile and artifice of hell,—
And human scorn, indignity, and shame,
Combin'd against Him, could infuse a stain
Of guilt or sin into His holy mind ;
His eye, omniscient, saw all wrath consum'd—
All righteousness fulfill'd, and vict'ry won ;
And with a voice of unexhaust'd might,
He loud proclaim'd, " 'Tis finish'd," and expir'd.

Mysterious God ! Thy word of mighty pow'r
A universe produc'd ; one glance of Thine
Could wipe it from Thy sight. Oh ! what could
    move
Thy sov'reign will to pity so sublime,
And sacrifice so vast, for sinful man ?

And sin ! how hateful to thy holy eye,
Wherever seen ? how dreadful its desert ?
More hateful now, more terrible its fruits,
In opposition to such wond'rous love ;
Salvation, oh, how precious !   Life regain'd
At such a price—what must its value be ?
Who would expend it on a paltry whim ?
Or try to fill it with aught less than God ?
Pause, oh my soul,—can faith survey the cross ;
The suff'ring Saviour ; the full sacrifice,
With all thy guilt thereon, and all consum'd ;
Full restitution made, and thee releas'd ;
Invested with new life, inducement, pow'r ;
Constrain'd by drawings of infinite love
To magnify the riches of His grace,
In sweet obedience to the great design
For which he stoop'd so low ?
Can Faith respond, by doings of the life ;
By active deeds of purity and love ;
And witness bearing to the truth divine ;
And earnest efforts to diffuse its sway ;
And upward reaching to all holiness,
In preparation for immortal spheres,
And endless triumphs in redeeming grace ?

　　Let awe conceal the conflict of the tomb,
Where He descended, glorious in His might ;
The mortal life resign'd,—a princely gift,—
Not the disposal of a will less great ;

All life in death, to meet the spoiler there,
And in the prowess of omnipotence,
Prone to great deeds, divest the dreaded foe
Of all his terrors to His ransom'd ones ;
And quench the prestige of his lengthen'd reign,
And bind him down a subjugated slave,
Subservient to His purposes of grace ;
To terminate the troubles of the just,
Curtail their trials, and at last release
From mortal strife to everlasting rest ;
To guard their slumbers during their repose,
Through intervening time, and wake them up,
By His reviving pow'r, to endless life.

The wound was fatal. Death was over-match'd,
And abject trembl'd in His mighty grasp ;
Till now unvanquish'd on terrestrial soil,
His dreary caves, where he had stalk'd so long
In peerless gloom and sullen solitude,
Felt the infusion of celestial hope,
And grew less gloomy, frightful, and abhorr'd ;
Its regions all, the Mighty One travers'd,
And cast the arms of ownership around
The slumb'ring dust of generations past ;
Impress'd thereon His seal of right and claim,
Against the doings of the final day.

Hence toiling pilgrims now can, undismay'd,
Through death's dark regions firmly plant the foot ;
Descend his gloomy vale ; feel his advance,

As step by step he stealthily draws near,
And tighter presses on the beating heart ;
Or, with a bound, enclasps the mortal frame,
And bears it to repose ; with calmness now
They hear his summons ; meet his ghastly glance ;
Resign themselves into his cold embrace ;
And slumber there in hope of coming day.
To humble faith his terrors all have fled ;
The gloomy grave,—gorg'd with putrescence vile,
And relics of mortality, unseal'd
To cheering rays from the celestial spheres,
Unfolds a passage through its dreary haunts,
To glorious portals of felicity.
Oh, ye redeem'd ! why shrink to enter there ?
You follow Him who trode its shady depths,
Whose vivid footprints may confirm your trust—
Whose high renown and fragrance still remain,
To be your shield and solace in its gloom.
  Angelic sentries, with astonish'd awe,
Beheld their Lord, in seeming weakness, yield
To death's embrace, and hang upon the cross,
And like a mortal sink into the grave,
The prostrate victim of o'erwhelming shame ;
Within whose regions light dare not intrude,
Save underiv'd, essential light alone ;
In holy wonder and profound amaze
They cluster'd round the mystery sublime ;
Then struck their muffl'd harps, and softly sung—

" How wonderful His works, His ways obscure ;
He walks amidst unsearchable designs,
Mysterious form'd ; His footsteps are unknown ;
Jehovah holy, holy, holy is !"
From higher climes responsive hosts replied—
" Jehovah holy, holy, holy is !
His glory fills the boundless universe !
Midst waters deep his paths are hid from view !
His glorious footsteps never can be known !"
Respond, Believer, in triumphant strains ;
'Tis now develop'd ; much is understood,
And bright'ning ever as existence speeds,
And pealing louder through the realms of bliss,
As souls redeem'd are gather'd into heav'n ;
And ever swelling the triumphant strain :—
" Jehovah holy, holy, holy is !
His gracious love is over all His works ;
We praise Him most—His blood was shed for us."

   Oh, raise the banner of the cross on high,
O'er every land ; above all Time's pursuits ;
The glorious symbol of a world redeem'd ;
The Gospel trumpet through creation sound,
To rouse the slumbers of earth's torpid sons,
And shake them loose from lying vanities ;
Arrest their vacant eye, and fix it there,
On that inscription, trac'd by love's life-blood :—
" Peace upon earth, and goodwill towards men."
Thence bid them look into the empty tomb,

Where Glory stoop'd, and Wisdom paus'd inert ;
Omniscience veil'd itself; Omnipotence
Reclin'd ; perfections all stoop'd down
To lowest depths, to raise the sinner up
From death, to life and immortality.

CHAPTER XII.

ARGUMENT.—Why the common Fear of Death?—The Quietness of the Grave.—In view of it, the vanity of Earthly Pursuits, and folly of anxiety about them.—The uses of Death.—The despondency of the Disciples at the Messiah's Death.—The Guard of Soldiers.—Their Occupation and Feelings unlike that of the Disciples.—The final discomfiture of Death.—His Flight.—The predicted period of Messiah's Resurrection arrives.—The security of His Enemies.—The dawn of the Day of Rest.—Its change indifferent. — Hypocritical Formality of His Enemies.

———

CHRISTIAN! why shrink from Death's advancing
    step?
Why so much pains to keep him at the door,—
To shun his stroke, and ward off his embrace,—
To gain a truce, though for a worthless hour,
Of pain, suspense, and racking misery?
Why plead and chaffer for a paltry breath,
Wrung from his avarice,—a feeble step,
A useless unit to the sum of life?
Another struggle in its vain turmoil,
Ere you retire to silence and repose?
   Hearts bleed not in the grave. Tranquillity

Surrounds its lonely tenantry. Each head
Is smoothly pillow'd there.   No thorns unseen
Engender pain into that silent couch ;
No dreams disturb ; no rude intruder breaks
With boisterous clamour into that retreat ;
To-morrow's cares breed no harrassing thoughts,
And grim foreshadows of perplexity,
To toss the bosom with disquietude ;
The greedy sleeper of a thousand years
Cleaves to his couch with undiminish'd zest.

Behold the change a moment may produce !
This instant grasping at a fleeting breath—
Another turn of the derang'd machine,
More precious than a throne ;—the next, asleep,
And only rous'd by the archangel's trump.
To-day, this life is all ; for it alone
What toil and trouble does the heart endure ?
Depress'd, elated, as its varying sky
Breaks into sunshine, or is wrapt in clouds ;
For ever scheming, vainly to rear up
Some glorious fabric on its shifting sand ;
In dread of death, because a moment hence
His touch may prove its vanity ; may snatch
The childish trifles of this passing scene ;—
Its vain ambitions, and its petty schemes,
And hide them out of sight, to raise the heart,
As eagle bears its unaccustom'd brood
From the firm eyrie in the lofty rock,

To spread the wing in more etherial climes.
Absorb'd with empty nothingness below,
The heart rejects reality above ;
And views suspicious the declining day,
And length'ning shadows of this mortal state ;
The more it has, the deeper its regret ;
Its trust the greater, so much more it feels
The separation ; as if 'twere its own,
To pamper self with luxury and pride.
Anticipations of the great assize,
And its account, should moderate desire,
And breed contentment with a humble lot,
And short possession of terrestrial good.

 Earth is delug'd with unavailing tears ;
Its sweetest music but a wail of woe ;
We cannot bear to see our toy remov'd,
Though it is marring ev'ry worthy joy,
And clouding all our prospects for the skies ;
Yet we must suffer to be told the truth,
To have its lessons urg'd on our regards,
Though it should sting us to the very quick :
So death, unwelcome, enters our abode,
Claims the sweet babe we fondly thought our
 own,
And rudely hides it from our doting view.
'Twas ours but yesterday—to-day, 'tis gone ;
And comfort we refuse, though well assur'd
That it is sav'd from many a devious course

Of sin and sorrow,—nay, from hell itself,
And has reach'd heaven by a shorter road.

We fail to learn. So death returns again,
And with a stroke unnerves the friendly arm,
Unstrings the loving heart, or stills the voice,
On which confiding, we had long repos'd,
And fondly trusted would support our steps
Amidst the struggles of increasing years ;
Now blighted prospects, fondly-cherish'd hopes,
And lofty schemes, are levell'd with the dust ;
Hence we complain, because our foolish dreams
Pass and evanish, by the touch of truth.

So felt the chosen few, when the huge stone
Lay broad and heavy on Messiah's tomb—
The lowly wreck of all their hope and trust ;
All His pretensions, with His mission, crush'd
Beneath the ban of the imperial seal.
Barbarian soldiers, true to their commands,
Kept wakeful vigils round the flinty rock,
To ward intrusion, and thus guard secure
The seeming success malice had achiev'd ;
Unconscious guards of Heaven's eternal truth,—
So oft impugn'd by enmity and crime ;
Unconscious, too, of their exalted trust,
While heedless pacing in familiar terms,
And jocund mood, in precincts of the tomb ;
Or straying far in meditative thought
To cherish'd homes, or radiant smiles of love,

And absent friends, and liberty, and peace ;
Reflecting not what more than mortal strife
Was now enacting in the silent tomb ;
Life match'd 'gainst Death within his own domain,
Each with the ardour of determin'd will,
Skill never thwarted, prowess unsubued ;
On whose success not doubtfully depends,
Man's future fate, and Heaven's supremacy.
They all unconscious pac'd their weary rounds,
Of fear devoid, or aught to interrupt
The listless musings of their lonely hours,
Or break the trust imperiously impos'd
With penal force on their fidelity ;
For all experience hitherto obtain'd
Assur'd the safety of the tenants there,
In full submission to the tyrant's sway.

No fears had they.   No hope the chosen few ;
Their carnal views and visionary hopes
Of earthly honour had been all dispell'd ;
The great Messiah, whom they thought design'd
To raise the splendour of an earthly throne,
And show'r on them distinction and renown,
In shame had perish'd, and was now no more—
The lowly tenant of the silent tomb ;
And left them nought but sorrow and regret ;
Their fervent trust, and reverence, and love,
Repos'd in worth transcendant and sublime,
Dispell'd so rudely, made their hearts recoil

In disappointment and regret ; while they,
In hopeless sorrow, bitterly complain'd : —
" We thought 'twas He who Israel should redeem."
   It was not so within that lonely tomb.
Though veil'd from sense in dim obscurity
The mortal frame, girt with omnipotence,
Corruption could not touch ; the greedy grave,
Appall'd custodier of perfection pure,
Quak'd to its centre, and drew back dismay'd ;
Death gasp'd convulsively at His approach,
And shunn'd encounter with the Prince of Life.
It was not conflict—'twas authority,
Resistless and supreme, laid on the foe,
That crush'd his prowess, and his courage quench'd ;
He felt th' unequal match, and all the plagues
Of dissolution siez'd his wonted might ;
In grim dismay he quit his ancient hold
Of mortal being, and resign'd his sway
Within the regions of the silent grave ;
In impotence and rage his lust coil'd up ;
And all his terrors shrunk within himself,
Unable to endure the crushing grasp
Of holiness divine. In abject shame,
And baffl'd rage, and envious regret,
Precipitate he fled, with all his brood,
To the abyss of darkness and despair ;
And left the spoils of generations past
To grace the triumphs of the Prince of Life ;

And his abodes of loneliness, and gloom,
And prostrate hopes, and lacerated hearts,
To be infus'd with light of coming joy.
  The hour had come, not doubtingly foretold
By the Redeemer, when He trode the earth ;—
Long since ordain'd in Wisdom's deep resolves,
Ere time existed, or a cause arose,
From sin admitted, or a creature form'd,
To know its evil, and its curse endure ;—
The hour of hell's discomfiture and shame ;
When all its malice, artifice, and wiles,
Recoil'd with fearful vengeance on itself ;
The hour of expectation 'mong the throng
Of awe-struck seraphs, in the abodes of bliss,
Intent to see the mystery unveil'd
That hung portentous o'er the Holy One,
And wrapt His glory in obscurity ;
To see the symbols of infinite wrath
Draw up appeas'd, in majesty serene,
And love unclouded, as of old it shone
Within the bosom of th' unmeasur'd past,
Resting in splendour on the Son belov'd,
With honour unimpair'd through ages all ;
To see sure tokens from th' Imperial Judge,
Of satisfaction render'd to His law,
In restitution of its injur'd worth ;
And the illustrious Substitute releas'd
From further obligation to its claims ;

From His debasement freed, with vict'ry crown'd,
And new-won honours, fruit of His exploits,
And lasting trophies of His matchless pow'r;
So wond'rously display'd on man's behalf,
And the diffusion of God's glorious grace.

Night's sombre shades, quiescent hanging o'er
The soothing slumbers of a busy world,
Were roll'd aside, to welcome the approach
Of smiling morn, with all her varied charms
(Long-hallow'd morn, whereon almighty pow'r
From mighty deeds abstain'd, and call'd it *rest*—
For names are nought, where thought is under-
    stood);
With glorious mission, never hers before—
To shed her beauties round a risen Lord,
And tranquillise grief's agitated tide,
With certain prospect of unfading joy,—
Drawn from the Cross, and from the empty tomb,
And Him who there sojourn'd; to soothe the
    heart
With living streams from Calv'ry's dying groans,
And bring it nearer to the living One,
To rest confiding on His precious death,—
And in the freedom which that death bestows,
Elastic bound to immortality.

That hallow'd morn its blushing sweets disclos'd;
And man, oblivious of his recent crimes,
And monstrous deeds of blood, had wash'd his hands

With sanctimonious care ; then formal walk'd,
The strictest course of Israel's paschal rite,
In mockery profane of its designs ;
Invok'd the God of Jacob ; kindred claim'd ;
The promise claim'd, and all that it conveys,
As theirs, in right of Heaven's unchanging choice,
And their observance of those rites obscure ;
The glory claim'd of great Messiah's reign,
In earthly power array'd, and thus exalt
To proud distinction their dejected race.
Lull'd to quiescence by their blinded zeal
And hollow pride of ancient privilege,
Men quietly slept, or, in uneasy dreams,
They re-enacted all their former crimes,
Invok'd the guilt upon their heads anew,
And on their offspring left the hideous stain,
(A legacy well earn'd by deeds their own) ;
Or, wakeful, plotted wickedness afresh,
To hide the guilt of deeds already done
Against Heaven's matchless love—reveal'd,
Procur'd, bestow'd, by the incarnate Son :
Fain to believe their hatred had consign'd
His high pretensions to oblivion,
And Him inclos'd for ever in the tomb.

CHAPTER XIII.

———

AROUND th' Imperial Tomb, in humble awe
And mute astonishment, seraphic hosts
Inquiring bent, with reverence profound,
To reach some views into th' amazing depth
Of self negation and humility,
To which Emmanuel stoop'd, when lo !
The greedy grave, unable to endure
The horrid plagues His presence made her feel,
In agony intense relax'd her hold
On generations past, fill'd with dismay,
By dread intrusion of celestial light,
That claim'd affinity to mortal dust,
And spoiled her revels among human skulls,

Maintain'd by her so long, but now renounc'd,
Or feebly held, obedient to His will,
To be restor'd on restitution's morn.

Unharm'd therein, untainted by decay,
Emmanuel burst the bandages of death ;
Shook off the grave, and rose again to life ;
Cast degradation off, and sin, and shame,
And all the badges of His low estate.
Mortality retir'd. His human frame—
The first ripe fruits of sleepers in the grave,
In life unfading, from celestial climes—
Was gorgeously array'd, fit to sustain
Unbounded honour, sov'reignty, and power
From heaven above, and from the earth below.
Imputed sin adher'd no more to Him :
Its dismal fruits for ever disappear'd ;
Justice divine was honour'd, and withdrew
Her catalogue of woes—all cancell'd now ;
Humiliation, sorrow, shame, disgrace,
No place could find for residence in Him ;
Sin, Death, and Hell, amidst perpetual plagues
And everlasting shame, conceal'd their rage ;
The human guards, in dread astonishment
And awe profound, fled with the strange report ;
Gave attestation to the wondrous fact ;
To His invet'rate foes unwelcome proof
Of bootless malice and atrocious crime.
He, glorious in His might, triumphant burst

Death's feeble band, till now invincible—
Which generations held in abject sway,
And shed the radiance of incipient life,—
Rays of Himself, infus'd into the dust
Of ages, shrouded in neglect,—and cloth'd
The ghastly tenants of the gloomy grave
In expectation's bloom, and light, and grace,
And hope divine, and promise most secure ;
And left behind the fragrance of His love,
His peace and seal of high authority,
And special claim to every slumb'ring one,
To smooth their pillow, sweeten their repose :
That all His chosen to the end of time,
When all the toils of pilgrimage have ceas'd,
In faith serene, might stretch their weary limbs,
And calmly rest till shadows flee away.

His train was Glory and transcendant Light,—
And Truth complacent in her brightest robes,—
And Peace exulting in her placid joy,—
And Love triumphant in her high exploits,—
And Wonder spread in curious amaze,
Like fleecy cloud around celestial hosts
And souls already won, (award bestow'd
By Him who ever is, and never knew
Contingency). 'Twas Mercy's crowning hour,—
When full completion rested on her schemes,—
When all her streams of goodness manifold,
So long restrain'd by righteousness and truth,

Flow'd like a torrent towards human kind,—
When hidden pity, with compassion, sung
Her sweetest strains of tenderness and joy,—
When all her secret longings and desires
Were fully realiz'd, and on her head
A crown, enrich'd with many precious gems,
Was placed in token of her high renown,
And she array'd in her essential charms
Of glowing sympathy, compassion, love,—
Was recognis'd, among perfections high,
Residing in Divinity alone,
In undiminish'd measure and degree ;
And in th' effulgence of innate delight,
And tranquil dignity supremely sweet,
She stretch'd her hand in confidence to Truth,
And heap'd her glory on the risen Lord.

And Truth inflexible, dissolv'd in smiles,
Forsook his injur'd mien and look severe,
Arose to gladness and development,—
Rose to the glory of acknowledg'd right,
And vindication from all wrong sustain'd ;
Resum'd his splendour and intensity,
His ancient honour and undoubted sway,
Among the doings of the universe ;
And in the lustre of unsullied fame,
And firm immutability, he join'd
In Mercy's tribute with approving joy,
And shed his glory on the risen Lord.

And Peace appear'd in placid dignity,
Radiant as light from th' eternal throne.
Resistless in her captivating grace,
She drew around her Heaven's ecstatic bliss
And all her sources of felicity,
And winning strains of glowing harmony,
That fills her countless harps with endless song,
And upward drew the founts of human thought,
Volition and desire to be solac'd
And blended with the melodies of Heaven,
Whence clouds of glory rose, and pendant
    hung,
To grace the fervour of her loveliness,
And fill her bosom with Divine perfume :
In these, exulting with complacent joy,
She shed her glory on the risen Lord.
    Justice beheld, and could demand no more,
His wonted frowns and rigorous demands,
Indignities endured ; redress withheld ;
Long catalogue of heinous wrongs sustained ;
Arrears long due,—now fully satisfied,
And honour paid to equity supreme ;
He raised his head in uprightness Divine—
Erect and stable as th' imperial throne,
In furbish'd rectitude invincible,
By satisfaction sweeten'd and subdu'd ;
Strict guardian of all right, acquir'd, bestow'd,
Or else inherent, he triumphant stood

In the full splendour of essential right,
Asserted, and retriev'd, and join'd with peace,
To shed his glory on the risen Lord.

Redemption rose, all perfect and complete,—
A new creation 'mong God's wond'rous works,—
Sprung from perfections hitherto unknown,
With functions new, and mission more sublime,
And more expressive of Almighty power ;
Resource more varied ; wisdom more acute ;
All excellence more manifest and pure,
And more attractive to created thought,
Than aught the boundless universe contains.
Its searchless glory dimmed all other lights ;
All princely being in celestial spheres
Concentrate gaz'd in wonder and delight
On its astonishing magnificence.
And when he bore the evidence on high,
That it was finish'd, as by compact fix'd,
Its boundless grace and riches all combin'd
To shed its glory on the risen Lord.

Almighty Power and Holiness, unstain'd
In undiminish'd energy, combin'd
Unmeasur'd effort with all high design,
Effect with purpose, impulse with result ;
Transfus'd through all volition, to secure,
By sway resistless over all events,
Designs and deeds, by creature will pursu'd ;
The full fruition of abounding grace

To each and all the chosen sons of light,
And shed its glory on the risen Lord.

All attributes divine,—known, or conceal'd
From finite vision, in the depths of light,—
Unsearchable,—conven'd in council deep,
And grave acceptance of His glorious work,
In attestation of the honour done
To each perfection of the great Supreme,
And revenue of glory thence secur'd
To the imperial throne; in full resolve,
Combin'd to dwell in residence complete,
As in the Godhead, so in manhood too,
In utmost fullness and complacency;
To guide all things, and to supply all grace,
And rule supreme—God-man for ever blest—
In recognition of His triumphs won.

Adoring angels hailed their risen Lord;
His wounds replete with glory, light, and love;
His Manhood radiant in divinity,—
Badge of His office in the courts above,
And bright memorial of amazing love;
His priestly vesture sanctified by blood,—
Perpetual proof of right to intercede,
With sov'reign power, before the mercy seat,
For the rewards of merit all His own.

They bore the tidings of His victory
To cheer the bosoms of His faithful few,
Plung'd into sorrow by His recent shame,—

To wake conviction of His mighty pow'r,
And truth unfailing, and identity ;—
The great Messiah, still in human form,
With all the sympathies of brotherhood,
To fill their hearts with confidence and peace.
Strange tidings these ! which confirmation need
By evidence most clear,—repelling doubt,—
Insuring highest credence of the heart ;
That so confirm'd, His servants might declare,
Before a hostile world, that it was so!

It was so done ; by attestation clear,
Which to reject involves absurdity.
Too gross for candid reason to admit,
Or highest art of malice to excuse.
Then He who stoop'd from Glory's lofty heights,
In willing converse with unfallen man,
Again convers'd in humble brotherhood,
And Friendship's loving tone,—replete with light,
In exposition of His empire new ;
Breath'd inspiration of celestial fire,
To clear their vision, and confirm their faith ;
Bequeath'd His peace, and promise full of grace—
His unseen presence ; and His Spirit felt,
In marv'lous pow'r, and light, and energy,
For mission high, as heralds of the Cross.

His mission ended, and His work complete,
He upward rose above this lowly vale,
And all memorials of mortality ;

Borne in chariot of Omnipotence,
Swift to the glory of His native climes,
Which outward spread to hasten His ascent,
He cleft the fleecy clouds.   The firmament
Roll'd up her splendid tapestry, and hung
In bright magnificence around ; on which
Unnumber'd zephyrs, wing'd with purest light,
And fragrant with perfume, attendant paus'd,
Like teeming myriads, honouring renown ;
Ten thousand legions of seraphic hosts,
In varied hues, and costume of the skies,
All in surpassing brilliancy and bliss,
In phalanx close, lined His imperial course
From climes terrestrial to celestial spheres.

The inner clouds of glory drew apart,
Refulgent with ineffable applause,
In pendent splendour shaded His approach ;
Bliss undisclos'd, in aromatic folds,
Elastic yielded to His viewless step,
And spread its odours o'er His joyous way.
All honour was His path ; tranquillity,
Light inaccessible, and majesty,
In meet devotion round His chariot hung ;
From the imperial throne, dominions, pow'rs,
Thrones, principalities, of ev'ry grade ;
Archangel, angel, cherubim,
And seraphim, in multitudes untold,—
Each in his fairest panoply adorn'd,

And golden harps with adoration strung,
And reverence profound,—stretch'd out to line
His bright advance with plaudits of renown.
The clefted clouds, with teeming multitudes,
In humble distance rang'd, recumbent bent
Beneath the pressure of ecstatic joy,
And rapturous applause ; while He drew near
To secret place of the Eternal One,
Amidst the glorious shouts, and holiest strains,
Of ev'ry harp throughout the mighty throng,
Such as ne'er rung in heavenly spheres before.
Infinite love, ineffable, supreme,
As in duration past, embrac'd the Son,
Complacent with unutterable delight ;
And all dominion, honour, majesty,
By seal immutable, was on Him laid,
As Mediator of Heaven's highest praise.
⸱ Attending myriads, on elastic wing,
Dim in excess of light, and numbers vast,
Before, behind, in orderly array,
Harp'd melody and praise in holiest strains,—
Resounding o'er the everlasting heights,
With loud hosannahs of enraptur'd bliss ;
Each peal succeeding, bursting more intense
With ecstacy sublime, and vivid thought
Of marv'lous doings in terrestrial climes.
Those in advance, in shouts to those behind,
In emulation holy, pealing forth :—

" Hosannahs, praise, dominion, power ascribe,
To the Redeemer of the human race !
All glory His ; all praise to Him belongs ;
Though David's son, yet David's mighty Lord ;
He left to conquer, now He comes to save.
Lift up your heads, ye everlasting gates ;
Ye doors enduring, be ye lifted up,
That He, the King of Glory, may come in."
Those in advance, in eulogistic strains,
On harps melodious, fraught with highest bliss,
That fill'd the portals of celestial climes,
Enquiring harp'd, evolving raptures new :—
" Who is this King of Glory ? who is this ?
So full of honour, majesty, renown,
Triumphing in His excellence and fame,—
That dims the lustre of seraphic spheres,
And nears the mansions of enduring bliss ?"
Harps numberless replied :—" Ev'n that same Lord
That great in might, and strong in battle is."
Vibration bore the onward peal along.
To clust'ring myriads at the pearly gates ;
The loud acclaim in swelling plaudits rung :—
" Lift up your heads, ye gates, ye bars draw back,
Ye doors of everlasting strength, on high
Be lifted up, that He, the mighty King
Of Glory, may come in."   To whom, again,
Their harps inquiring, speedily return'd :—
" Who is the King of Glory ? who is this ?"

To whom replying, countless echoes sped : —
" Ev'n that same Lord who in essential might
Trode the fierce winepress of infinite ire ;
Sustain'd the onslaught of all hostile foes,
In regions vile, with base apostacy,
And drove them headlong to the gulf of woe,—
To chains of darkness and infinite wrath ;
In new-won lustre, from apparent shade,
Enrob'd the sov'reign government and will
With vindication, glorious and pure,
And glory brighter than when unassail'd.
Behold, He comes ! with trophies of His might ;
With full redemption, and with many crowns
For souls redeem'd, to reap eternal joy.
He comes from deep debasement, to resume
His wonted throne of majesty supreme,—
To rule the empire purchas'd with His blood."
    Immortal rapture holier seem'd to rise ;
And everlasting joy, in mighty floods,
Roll'd their transparent torrents round the throne;
Array'd in holiness serene, and truth, and love,
For the reception of the mighty One ; .
Pow'rs, thrones, dominions, lights of ev'ry hue,
And glory various, concentrate rush'd,
In humble order, reverent, devout,
On adoration's wing ;—a noiseless throng
Of countless hosts, to view Divinity,
Now made apparent in the human form.

Surpassing wonder thrill'd through ev'ry breast,
And simultaneous burst from ev'ry harp,—
Like noise of many waters, rising high
Above the perfum'd atmosphere of light,
In loudest praises to His holy name.

   Oh ! for a place among the glorious throng,
Whose songs have never ceas'd, nor harps been
   mute !
Remote, obscure, unnotic'd,—yet a place ;
And humble harp, and skill to touch its strings,
Though least melodious ; rude, but yet in tune ;
To sound one note,—one everlasting strain
Of quenchless gratitude to sov'reign grace,
That gave that life a sacrifice for me !

CHAPTER XIV.

IN court supreme,—as Deity conven'd
Within the secrets of essential light,
Ere man was form'd,—so now ; from finite view
Conceal'd in glory inaccessible,
Save by divulgence of the will divine ;
All attributes appear'd which Godhead owns,—
Those known to mortals, those to angels too ;
Those undisclos'd—if such there be—apart
From finite intercourse, or else too pure
For gross conception of created mind,
Where its rude vision vainly tries to search ;—
All there assembl'd in acknowledgment,
And just expression of complacency,
And high approval of the merit won.
  Omniscience rose, and all His deeds detail'd ;
Describ'd His travail, agony, and woe,--

His dread amaze, astonishment, and grief,—
The wrath He bore,—the anguish, insult, shame ;
His firm endurance,—His negation dire, -
And mighty conflict with malignant foes ;
His glorious triumphs,—all His victories ;
His spoils from death, and trophies from the grave ;
Hell's subjugation, shame, discomfiture ;
Sin's sway defeated, and its end secur'd,
In terms of compact, perfect and complete—
Full restitution of invaded good.

The Law Divine unroll'd its code of Life ;
Its forfeiture by man,—by man restor'd ;
Its terms compar'd with restitution made,
And gladly own'd acceptance of the deed ;
Withdrew its tale of wrongs, so long endur'd, .
Wrapt up its countless claims—all now fulfill'd,
And smil'd serene in rectitude and peace ;
Its high behests with vindication crown'd,
Now bas'd upon integrity and truth,—
Entrench'd within the ramparts of the Cross ;
Arose to honour and authority,
In view of all intelligence ; receiv'd
Acknowledgment and due regard ; and thence
Own'd satisfaction, and itself appeas'd.

And Justice rose, resplendent in his light
And stern inflexibility, in smiles serene ;
Benignant roll'd his ire within itself,
And sheath'd his flaming sword, and rais'd his voice,

In attestation of the ransom paid
For restoration of degraded man;
And shut the gate to regions of despair,
And plac'd his seal upon its musty bars;
Securing Him, and all His chosen ones,
From penal risk of sin's malignity;
Resign'd the charter to enduring life
Into Emmanuel's hands, without reserve,
As high custodier of all privilege,
Provision, gifts, and influence and grace,
To cleanse, uphold, and elevate the soul
For meet probation in terrestrial climes,
Or high perfection in celestial spheres.

And Truth arose; review'd the ancient pledge,
Propos'd, accepted, in the Triune mind,—
The full conditions specified therein;
To which the Son, as substitute, adher'd,
For God's high honour, and for man's relief;—
All true obedience, to the full extent
Of man's divergence from integrity;
And full submission to the penalty
Of disobedience and apostacy:
These he review'd, in his own piercing light,
And tested them with high perfection's code;
And now declar'd all righteousness fulfill'd,—
The ransom paid with an unsparing hand;
No jot omitted; not a pang unborne;
Or deed undone that was requir'd from man;

K

Declar'd concurrence in His just rewards ;—
His right to hold, and to communicate,
To whom he wills, the favours He has won ;—
Abounding grace and energy divine ;
All light and knowledge ; all support and aid ;
Endearing union ; sonship with Himself,
To all who own Him as their Lord and King :
Then in unsullied purity adorn'd,
As in refulgence of primeval grace,
Himself He gave,—in oracles Divine,
And understanding of their grave import,
To guide His chosen to the Land of Rest.

Then Wisdom deep, of all device appris'd,
Shone glorious in the consummated work,
And now embrac'd its manifold results,—
All high disclosures of the mind Divine,
And precious fruits to creatures of His hand,
Concentrate in, or emanating from,
The wond'rous scheme, so wond'rously achiev'd ;—
Its twofold bearing, pregnant with rich fruits
To God and man ; securing, as of old,
To God His glory, and to man his God ;
Revealing God, in excellence supreme,
Exalted on a pinnacle of worth
And high attraction, never known before,
Among the myriads subject to His sway—
Cloth'd with compassion, yet all holiness ;
Whom finite creatures, ever prone to err,

May ever trust, and imitate, and love.
Then to Messiah gave the book of fate,—
The ultimate disposal of all deeds ;
Control of all designs in freedom form'd
By finite will ; and unrestrain'd, pursu'd ;—
Gave record of all deeds, and their results,
In favour, or obstructive of His work,
With all their hues, diversities, and aims,
To further, or prevent, as seem'd Him good,
For the promotion of His great designs.
　Then Holiness, degraded and abjur'd,
And all but banish'd from terrestrial climes,
Now re-instated on her rightful throne,
And re-admitted into human hearts,
And by the Cross declar'd inviolate,
With vindicated majesty, up rose,
Bright in the honours of atoning blood,
Conven'd the secret agents of his sway ;—
The blessed Spirit, with resistless power,
And influence unseen, and precious seeds,
And distillations of abounding grace,
To rear up souls to full maturity ;
To open hearts, and loosen silent tongues,
To magnify the riches of His grace,
And placed them all into Messiah's hands,
In attestation of His matchless worth.
　Mercy, exulting in her high exploits,
And the completion of long cherish'd hopes,

In high convention rang'd, and council deep,—
Maintain'd untarnish'd by Emmanuel's work,
And plac'd them all upon His glorious head.
Then in His hands, in virtue of that work,
And terms of ancient covenant, bestow'd
Entire possession, for Himself alone ;
And for behoof of all redeemed ones,
All light, and wisdom, motive, influence ;
All peace, and hope, and aspiration pure ;
All gracious streams ; the Spirit's mighty power,
To train a people for His endless praise ;
Celestial crowns, and everlasting thrones ;
Eternal mansions ; palms of victory ;
Unfading pleasures ; unalloy'd bliss ;
Ecstatic raptures that can never pall ;
All precious pleasures and extreme delights,
And princely gifts unseen by mortal eye,
By ear unheard, by bosom unconceiv'd ;—
Conferr'd all on Him, as the great High Priest
Of fallen man, within the courts above ;
One nature holding all Divinity,
The other circling round the church below,
And being all reposing on His arm.

  'Tis but a feeble echo of His praise,—
Beyond conception and all utterance,—
A dim, dark shadow of His glory vast,
That fallen mortals can endure to view ;
Yet how o'erpow'ring is its dimest ray !

What then the splendour of its cloudless blaze ?
Oh, for a seraph's piercing glance to know
And revel 'midst the glory all His own !
Heaven's holiest mansions rang with His applause ;
From host to host His wonders were proclaim'd ;
Till through th' enraptur'd realms of Paradise
No tongue was silent, nor a heart unmov'd,
By thrilling admiration of His deeds.
  Nor were those mute.   'Midst universal praise,
Redeem'd from earth and base mortality,
And borne on high by His amazing love,
They showed their many scars, and grievous
   wounds ;
Describ'd their degradation and escape ;
Their weakness, worthlessness, and crimes ;
And sought the lowest seats of copious bliss,
And humbly wonder'd how they had got there.
With harps of fuller tone, and more devout,
In deeper thrills of gratitude and love,
Attun'd to holier rapture, and inspir'd
By love's emotion, more intensely sweet,
They humbly hymn'd the glories of His grace.
  Astonish'd seraphs, in amaze, restrain'd
The full expression of their loud acclaim,
To catch the fervour of those grateful strains,
And learn the ardour of their humble joy ;
Then harp'd anew, in melody sublime,
All hallow'd glory to Jehovah's name,

Till thrones triumphant thrill'd with the excess ;
And, trembling 'neath exuberance of bliss,
They echoed back the raptur'd cadence far,
Resounding outward to the climes of earth :—
  "Salvation, glory, honour, power be His ;
All wisdom, blessing, riches, strength, and might,
Dominion, majesty, belongs to Him ;
Above all kings, dominions, potentates,
Supreme o'er all supremacy, he sits
In dignity his own, by merit won ;
All are His due, who by His own right hand
Subdued rebellion, and the mighty crush'd.
Praise Him, ye heav'nly hosts, princes, and pow'rs,
Ranks, dignities, of ev'ry grade and name,
Whose highest glory is to do His will ;
Praise Him, thou glorious sun, and silv'ry moon ;
Praise Him, ye countless stars, bright orbs of night,
Sparkling in depths of vast immensity ;
All lesser lights, that twinkle on the verge
Of distance indistinct, with all your tribes,
Sustain'd by impulse of His mighty hand,—
Oh ! magnify and praise His glorious name !
All elements combine His name to praise ;
Ye stormy winds, and gentle fanning breeze,
And boundless ocean, rivers, lakes, and streams ;
Fire, hail, and snow, exalt His glorious name.
Let sentient being join the loud acclaim ;
Fowls, soaring high, or nestling in the shade

Of mazy foliage, in plaintive song,
Or cooing love, or rich melodious strains ;
Ye bestial tribes, in wood, or wilderness,
Or noxious swamp, or boundless prairie,
Both great and small, ferocious or tame ;
Ye fishes, sporting in the restless deep,
Or listless dozing on the sunny banks,
Or stealthy creeping in the slimy marsh,—
Your pow'rs unite to magnify His praise.
Praise Him all nations, kings, and princes all ;
Judges and people, savage and refin'd ;
Both rich and poor, exalted and debas'd ;
Both old and young ;—extol His boundless praise.
Let saints on earth join the redeem'd above,
In hallelujahs to His glorious name."
Their swelling raptures, and unfading crowns,
And shining robes, wash'd in atoning blood—
By faith embrac'd, or else by sense enjoy'd—
Before His footstool cast, in homage due,
And adoration, and excess of joy.
And hosts redeem'd, in glorious response,
Burst into holier anthems to His name. :—
" The praise be His ; all glory is His due ;
Enduring honour, blessing, and renown ;
All adoration, gratitude, and love.
All the emotions of our ransom'd souls
Is cold return for His amazing grace,—
His own already, upon us bestow'd,—

'Tis all His own, for He was slain for us ;
We will extol and magnify His name
While being lasts, to thrill with endless bliss.
Oh ! for ten thousand cloven tongues of fire,
And hearts enflam'd, to utter all His praise !
Oh ! matchless love ! ineffable delight !
Exhaustless, quenchless, ever-during love !
In gushing floods of ravishment and joy,—
A weight of glory crushing to the sp'rit
By finitude begirt,—that only is endur'd
By grace sustaining, from His hand supplied.
Oh ! what is this ! embrac'd by love divine !
Launch'd on the ocean of perpetual bliss,
That rolls its tide of glory and delight,—
Increasing rapture and ecstatic joy,
To ravish spirits, only fit for death,
With life immortal, through atoning blood."

CHAPTER XV.

MUTE be the tongue, and hush'd the impious
    heart
In dreary blindness to its highest good,
That sneers and scoffs at the amazing tale
Of love redeeming—mercy to the vile—
And all their fruits, as things incredible ;
As deeds unworthy of the Holy One,
And far beneath the name and dignity
Of high supremacy.   Treats the results
As meagre and inadequate ; and thence
Evincing waste of energy and skill,
Unworthy of the Agent and His pains ;
Prodigious labour yielding small return.

   Nay, look abroad ; behold the countless spheres,
Where lavish care and goodness overflows,—
Where endless beauty, wealth, and harmony,

Each one adorns, and gilds the glorious whole ;
Which with a tongue of eloquence proclaim
The vast resources resident in Him
Who framed them all, and loaded ev'ry one
With proofs and exhibitions of Himself.
Creation all is teeming with His praise ;
And Providence responds, from ev'ry orb,
And ev'ry thing that moves and breathes therein,
With voice most clear, and audible, and plain,
The fact of His surpassing majesty.

But, crush the light of the least brilliant orb,
Or lure it off into a devious tract,
Beyond the regions of its Maker's care ;
The residue, however glorious,
Magnificent, and pure, is but a part ;
It leaves the rest a fragmentary thing,
That only yields a partial meed of praise :
Part only given, where the whole is due.

Yon glim'ring speck, perch'd on the verge of
    space,
That seems to shed a doubtful ray of light,
To prove existence 'mong created things,
Yet owns a kindred origin and aim
With brightest spheres, pois'd nearest to the throne,
Beneath the eye of the great Architect,—
Has felt the force of impetus divine ;
Basks in the sunshine of unceasing care,
And yields its tribute to Jehovah's praise.

Were it extinguish'd by a foeman's hand,
Its lustre quench'd, its harp forever hush'd ;—
Perfection's work is marr'd—is incomplete.
Strains universal can no more be heard ;
A perfect tribute is no longer giv'n ;
And high Omnipotence must now accept
A partial homage—where the whole is due.

   Nay, should that orb, by adverse impulse urg'd,
Stray from its course, into the wilds of space ;
Renouncing law, break up the common bond,
And settl'd equilibrium of the spheres ;
What sad collisions, ruin, and distress,
Would sweep creation into wreck and woe,
And shroud the glory of Omnipotence !
Where now the worth that claims all reverence ?
The wond'rous pow'r that form'd ? the wisdom,
   skill,
And goodness manifold ? All compromis'd
By one defect, most insignificant
Among the least of His exalted works ;
Bring back the wand'rer, and adjust his course ;
Make evil good ; undo the spoiler's work ;
Arrest confusion in its wild career ;
Cause order reign harmonious as before.
Then has Perfection fix'd a deeper seal
Of vast resource, alternative, device,
On all His works than was before display'd.

   God might have cast the worthless thing away,

And reign in undiminish'd sov'reignty,
Amidst the glory of unswerving spheres ;
Or made another to fill up the void,
And knit its frame with tendons more compact,
To move harmonious with the great machine.
His mind, prolific of all high device,
Could choose unerring, from unnumber'd schemes,
To clear the obscuration of His name ;
But in them all admission is involv'd
Of failure in construction or design,—
A contradiction not to be endur'd
In the all-perfect and unerring One.
Give restoration ; good from evil bring ;
Give pow'r and fervour to the frigid thing,
To blaze anew in its once darken'd sphere ;—
A deed more glorious thus will be achiev'd,
Than by its first production was display'd.

Just so with man.   God could have swept the
    earth,
And all its contents, to oblivion,
And form'd anew more upright hearts to fill
The vacant sphere of man's apostacy ;
Or else transfer, from some untainted clime,
Some tested child of rectitude and light,
To people earth, and re-awake its praise.
This might have been ; another race produc'd,
Begirt with pow'r to magnify His name,
And mingle hymns of gratitude and love,

In chorus full with all intelligence ;
While He, supreme—from diminution free—
Unmov'd by the defection of mankind—
Reviewing all, could still pronounce them "good."
Yet, 'midst the universal jubilee,
One harp is mute,—one strain remains unheard,
And imperfection rests upon the whole.
A wail of discord, fraught with failure, falls
In deep dissonance on the Almighty's ear.
Will Power and Wisdom willingly submit
To such necessity ?—would it be weak,
Undignified, or mean, to heal the breach,
And string the harp anew ?   Nay ; it is power,
To place the finger on the adverse spot,
And tone it up to melody and truth ;
The less it seems, His wisdom more is seen ;
When solv'd the problem never solv'd before,—
How sinful man may in His sight be pure,
And feel constrain'd, by His abounding grace,
To harmonise with all His glorious works.

CHAPTER XVI.

WITH honour crown'd, Emmanuel fill'd the throne
Of universal pow'r and majesty ;
Into His hands all providence was plac'd,
And all provisions of His purchas'd grace ;
The Spirit's pow'r, subservient to His will,
Co-equal else, acknowledg'd Him supreme,
And took direction from His high behests,
For the fruition of His glorious work.

So from the Cross a new creation sprung,
With seals more vivid of consummate skill,
And wisdom more sublime, and boundless pow'r,
Exhaustless goodness, and surpassing love,
Than all creative might elsewhere display'd.
A mustard seed, cast in th' ungenial soil

Of human passion, barrenness, and hate,
To rear its head, and spread its branches out,
O'er all humanity ;—their hearts refine ;
Their savage rites and horrid customs change ;
Dispel their selfishness ; and make the world
More habitable ; teach them how to seek
For pleasures fitting their high destiny.

Much has been done earth's darkness to dispel,
And light is spreading with no doubtful step ;
Tardy it seems to saints' impatient view,
But swift its progress in the sight of Heaven.
Empires will rise and fall, race follow race ;
Each child of Adam must probation bear—
Make his selection, manifest his will,
To rise to Heaven, or to perdition fall.
Time's course must run ; events must be matur'd,
Like the commotions of th' electric cloud ;
So combinations 'mong the human race—
Disjunctions too, advancement, and decay,
Must test its feelings towards grace divine,
Before the consummation can appear ;
But all events in Wisdom's hands remain.
The great High-Priest, who bends them to His
      will,
Well knows His own, and casts His chain of love,
In darkest times, around some hidden ones,
To draw and bind them to eternal bliss.

Much has been done earth's darkness to dispel,
No hour is barren of those high results;—

L

Each adds its jewels to the Saviour's crown ;
The ransom'd gather, as time flies apace
And will increase, through generations all,
Till it grows feeble, and in dotard age
Yields up its burden to eternity ;—
Till the last trophy of abounding grace
Is sought, and found, and gather'd into life.
The last is precious,—none is left behind,—
Time waits for him,—he has a place on high,—
His own fix'd beauty in Emmanuel's crown,—
A lustre his no other can emit ;
His voice, though weak, has its peculiar strain,
And is requir'd to make the chorus full
And melody complete ;—so time delays,
As angel tarried on Gomorrah's plains
Till lingering Lot was ready to depart.
The vile are safe till then, and may sin on,
In uncheck'd lust.   Wrath pauses in its ire,
And will not strike till that neglected saint
Is safely gather'd to his Father's house.
Oh, sinner ! gently treat Christ's chosen ones,
Less rudely thrust them in the world's turmoil ;
They screen you from the terrors of the Lord,
And for a space arrest your fatal doom.

    The last one sav'd, then Time's appointed course,
With all its doings, are for ever clos'd ;
A high Archangel on the rim of earth,
With arm uplifted o'er the broad expanse

Of land and ocean, swears by the Supreme
Who ever lives, " That Time shall be no more !"
And lifts his trumpet to earth's canopy,—
Through every clime proclaiming the fell doom,
That wraps up Nature among things that were.
All elements to dissolution fall ;
Polluted Earth, sad theatre of crime,
And guilt, and woe, melts with devouring flame ;
The Grave, distended into monstrous shape,
With surfeit of mortality, in terror quakes,
And to perdition flies.   Death, long disgrac'd,
Retires unbidden from his hated post,
So near the portals of immortal bliss,
And hides itself in the abyss of woe ;
And nought remains of all that once had been,
But human forms, emerging from the wreck,
Like the wing'd insect from its chrysalis,
Now to renew their interrupted bond
With vital being and intelligence,
And reap th' awards of an enduring state.
    The dead in Christ rise first ; the honour theirs
Of first release to freedom,—first escape
From the disasters of a flaming world,—
First entrance into life—refined, recast
Into the texture of seraphic spheres ;
All malformation gone ; inaptness fled ;
Disinclination, incapacity,
With time's debasements, have all disappear'd ;

Replac'd by beauty, symmetry, and grace—
All fitting gifts to form a residence
And glorious helpmate for the perfect soul.
No laggard there is seen ; not one hangs back
In weary weakness or suspicion's doubt ;
By welcome summons drawn, they come
From every clime and tongue,—a mighty host,
Which none can number but their living Head,—
Who has them written in his Book of Life,—
Each one array'd in robe of brightest hue ;
Like floating stars, they upward buoyant rise,
On exultation's wing, beyond the spheres.
. Ascending saint, say, Is your triumph full !
See, in amazement, how yon floating clouds
More glorious become, and brighter still,
Till Heaven seems in a blaze of ravishment
And light o'erwhelming, unless aid is giv'n ;
Descending glory spreads its massy folds
To vision's utmost bounds ; more dense it seems,
Exceeding all excess, as it draws near.
Upon their summit sits the Son of Man,
In bright effulgence of essential bliss,
And dignity supreme.   He comes to greet
His ransom'd ones to His enduring bliss.
Seraphic hosts, in ecstacy devout,
With humble awe adoring throng around ;
Saints, in surprise, caught from the contest hot,
With powers of darkness 'midst the world's pursuits,

And saints triumphant, long in rapture cloth'd,
Spread o'er the midway plain, in multitudes
Out-numb'ring number,—(convocation vast!)
Drawn by resistless love,—hail His approach
With high acclaim, and songs of Paradise,
And shouts of triumph, echoing through space,
One vast and universal jubilee :—

    " Behold He comes ! To judge the world comes
       He !
He is our King, for Him we've tarried long !
All eyes behold Him ! those who Him contemn'd
Shall be dismay'd at His dread Majesty.
Oh, what is this ?—conception fails to grasp
The full amount of glory realis'd,—
A risen Lord for ever to adore !
Faith lost in sight ! Hope to fruition brought !
And triumph crowning every earthly cross !
Away His travail, agony, and pain !
Away the crown of thorns, the robe of shame,
The foul reproach, derision, hate, and scorn,
Humiliation deep, imputed guilt,
The bloody sweat, the scourge, the cross, the grave,
And all the badges of mortality !
Come, Glory, all be His ! unutter'd praise !
All honour and renown, and power and might,
All adoration ever to Him pay !
He lives,—was dead,—and lives for evermore.
Farewell the grave, and all its dread alarms !

And farewell sorrow, sin, corruption, pain !
All weakness too, farewell ! all trouble, grief,
Despondency, and doubt—with all the ills
Of weeping, erring, frail mortality !
Farewell, sweet hope ! the harvest now is our's.
And farewell, faith ! our's is the promis'd land.
Thou chast'ning rod, farewell ! we stray no more.
Ye rip'ling streams of grace, the fount is our's !
Our's are the pleasures that can never fade !"

He comes, admired of all that in Him trust ;
The throne of judgment for Him is prepared,
And He, the Judge, in majesty His own,
And His imperial Sire's, sits down,
With dooms perpetual hanging on His word—
Its pillars truth, its light omniscience,
And its decisions perfect righteousness.
Around Him stand, in orderly array,
All holy tribes, in reverence profound,
Obedient messengers of His behests ;
Unfalt'ring wisdom, all authority,
Encircle Him with dignity supreme.

The Books are open'd ;—record of all deeds ;
Wherever done—in secret shades of night,
Or in the blaze of notoriety ;
By whomsoever done : by earth's proud peers
And self-appointed umpires of the race,
Whom but to doubt, or question, or gainsay,
'An insult was which life could not repair ;

Or her dejected sons, whose voice was hush'd,
Amidst the silence of obscurity ;—
The deeds of all who own'd the human name—
Their nature, object, tendency, result,
To forward or obstruct celestial truth,
And sweet obedience to the will divine ;
The worth of each, or else its hue of guilt
And base divergence from integrity ;
To each the motives and inducements given,
Or the resistance to be overcome ;
To vice, restraint ; to virtue, timely aid :
The rapid progress in perdition's course,
And fatal blindness to the nearing doom
Of shame and woe, that ever denser grows,
And waits to seize th' impenitent at last ;—
The saints' sore struggles for the crown of life,
Amidst temptations, weakness, doubts, and fears ;
The wounds they bore ; the insults they sustain'd ;
The shame despis'd ; the tortures they endur'd ;
Their perseverance, conquests, and defeats ;
Their silent labours, unacknowledg'd toils,
And witness-bearing in a hostile world,
And secret conflict with indwelling sin ;—
All burst instinctive into open light,
In record kept, as jewels to their crown,
And swell the tide of honour, peace, and joy,
On them conferr'd by the impartial Judge.

   What strange disclosures rise ! The first in name

And honour held among the sons of men,—
And often, too, ev'n in the house of God,
In gifts unequall'd, fir'd with quenchless zeal,
That rous'd to thought full many a wayward
    heart,—
Prov'd but a trumpet in the Spirit's hand,
Whose warning giv'n was quickly cast aside
Scarce recognis'd therein, without one trace
Of deed unselfish done for God alone.
That abject one, unknown beyond the cot
Which gave him shelter from the blasts of heav'n,—
Child of neglect, and bosom friend with grief,
With scarce a place within the church below,
Nor dar'd presume to own the Christian name,
Yet felt it safest to be near the Cross ;
And lov'd his Bible for its cheering light ;
And lov'd the Sabbath for its sacred rest ;
And lov'd its praises for their soothing strains ;
Imbib'd unwittingly their heavenly tone,—
Unconscious stole along the narrow path ;
He now, astonish'd with excess of bliss,
Lifts up his head among the ransom'd throng,
And loudest hails the coming of his Lord.

    What crimson deeds defile that truthful page,
In record held from ages long extinct,
To meet their workers on the day of doom !
What secret vice and open violence,
And vile oppression, tyranny, and wrong !

What sick'ning lists of perfidy and hate,
And lawless passion and profanity,
Of enmity to Heaven and strife with men,
Are written there, awaiting their release,
To fill the culprits with unutter'd woe!
Ambitious dupes! the scourges of mankind,
Drunk with oppression's blood, who upward rose,
With callous heart, through human groans and
    tears,
To giddy heights on pinnacles of time,
Where, unrestrain'd by fear of God or man,
They might compete for black supremacy
With the abandon'd spirits of the pit,
And scaith the world with their iniquity.
Time's misnam'd heroes, foremost in the strife;
The rude red savage with his hundred scalps,
Or wholesale homicide (what matters which)
Inspir'd by the fierce war-cry to despise
The widow's wail of misery and woe,
And for renown made butchery an art,
Devis'd a mode, by scientific rules,
Of crowding mortals to their last account,
When least prepar'd for such a scrutiny,—
Forestalling Heaven of his prerogative,
Of life, and death, and vengeance—only his.
The regal pomp, and strains of slavish praise,
Fame's loud acclaim, the halo of renown,
The mimic glory and the petty power,

Which then encircl'd their exalted heads,
Are bootless now to awe the righteous Judge,
Or silence one deep feeling of remorse,
Or steel the naked soul against despair.

The life's deeds *all* are there! Illustrious crimes
Can not eclipse the base divergent act
Of household tyrant or perfidious friend,
Who needs but space and more capacity,—
A larger sphere for more atrocity,
To place him foremost in the downward race.
Nor can the saint, who meets a martyr's crown,
Eclipse the hidden faith, and deeds obscure,
The secret love, the cup of water given ;
The silent help, advice, encouragement,
Or worthless mite of Christ's neglected ones ;—
The doubtful act by custom long allow'd,
Adroitly sanction'd by the aim in view,
Expertly clasp'd 'mong duty's sacred deeds,
Or veil'd by plea of weak infirmity,
Or pressing straits and dire necessity,
Assumes their just demerit and award ;
Nay, thoughts spontaneous, which unbidden rose,
And were crush'd back with terror and alarm,
Or foster'd into life and active deed,
For good or evil, recognition meet,
And have a place upon that open page.

The record, too, of great Jehovah's name,
Reveal'd to man, to woo him to the skies ;

His right to reign, His sov'reignty and power ;
His wisdom, goodness, and beneficence ;
His strong compassion for our erring race,
And wealth and will to bring them back to peace.
Inscrib'd on all His works, that they might read,
And from His doings learn the doer's worth,
Most clearly trac'd, in bright magnificence,
Upon the starry framework of the sky,
For ever glowing with infinite skill ;
Trac'd on the teeming earth, through all her
    spheres ;
On arid deserts and eternal snows,
And fertile plain and forest, hill and dale,
And caverns deep, and mountains' summits high ;
On bubb'ling stream and ocean's vast abyss ;
Writ on the sunbeam and the lightning flash ;
On rolling thunder, earthquake, cataract ;
And storm and calm, and Nature all inscrib'd,—
To win attraction to the Good Supreme.
On vital being, too, both weak and strong,
That roams the desert, skims the aerial clouds,
Or sports incessant in the briny deep ;—
With wond'rous beauty on the human frame,
And matchless wisdom on the soul within,
Strung and adjusted clearly to respond
To faintest touch on its mysterious chords.
On all events inscrib'd by prescient light,
Forecasting each into subserviency

To highest good, and wisdom's noblest ends ;
Prescribing bounds to nations, peoples, tribes,
Their rise and fall controlling at His will ;
Each like a bubble on the flowing stream—
This moment dancing in the sunny ray,
Unconscious onward by the torrent swept ;
The next exploded, and again absorb'd.
The varied lot of ev'ry member, too,
Attests His presence, goodness, love, and care,
His sphere and rank ; the work to him assign'd ;
His strength to do it if the will is there ;
The weight and measure of the burden borne ;
The help to bear it, and to make it light ;'
Are His appointments, and all speak of Him.
Inscrib'd most clearly on the sacred page—
Full exposition of creation's voice—
Proclaim'd in every land, to every race,
Though faint it seem'd, while yet the fading rays
Of Eden's glory linger'd on the world,
More bright it grew, more definite and clear,
Till the meridian dim'd all lesser lights,
And in its beams made every record plain.
The record, too, of privilege and gifts ;
The rich provisions of abounding grace ;
The light and knowledge, faculties and powers,
And spheres provided for their hallow'd use ;
The mercies furnish'd, the chastisements sent,
The invitations, promises, and calls,

The warnings, threat'nings, and persuasions too ;
The secret dealings of the Spirit's hand,
In application of the outward means,
Nor in assistance to expected deeds ;
Exact detail, and total sum of all ;
And how embrac'd, exerted, and improv'd,
Or else neglected for all saving good.
  No age nor clime could total darkness plead ;
Nor light too feeble, if the will was bent
To seek the truth, and in it refuge take ;
Each had its witness for the God of heav'n :-
Things visible proclaim'd the unseen One,
And pointed upward to sustaining pow'r
As fit to bless the spirits he had form'd ;
And hearts there were who could the lesson read,
In proof that others might have look'd, and liv'd ;
Primeval light led Abel to the skies,
And was as near to ev'ry soul besides ;
Good Noah's light was patent to the world ;
And Moses' God all Egypt must have known ;
The eastern Magi, untaught shepherds too,
Found the long-promis'd Child,—then Isr'el's king,
And waiting tribes, if willing, might have found ;
Rome's soldiers could decern—her sages might ;
The Grecian jailor saw—why not her judge ?
If lesser means could reach the way of life,
'Twas willing blindness made the greater fail.
On all the heights and highways of the world

Lights have appear'd to lead to endless rest ;
From ev'ry age are ransom'd ones conven'd,
In attestation of persistent grace,
And spotless rectitude of Heaven's awards
To deeds of darkness and impenitence.

What histories are there! Stript of the mask
And flimsy cov'rings with which time conceal'd
Its fatal frauds upon the human heart,
The uncloth'd spirit must in joy or shame
Stand side by side with its full tale of deeds,
Expos'd and trac'd to their extreme results ;
Must recognise the immatur'd designs
And vile conceptions entertain'd in time
As all its own, begotten of itself,
And will not be disown'd. Thought cannot die ;
For good or ill, it is a vital spark
That must increase into a quenchless flame,
And still expand while being onward rolls.
The ruling passion, artfully conceal'd
'Midst palliations and professions false
From human scrutiny,—nay, from the view
And observation of the sense within,
Till the deceiver is himself deceiv'd,—
Is now reveal'd in all it hideous hues.
The darling lust, nurs'd with a lover's care ;
The secret grudge, of envy or dislike ;
The impious thought, insinuation, jest,
Or lewd desire, deep cherish'd in the heart,

And overtop'd with many a specious deed,
Enshrouds their owner in astonishment,
When time's distinctions, honours, and renown,
Have lost their charms and faded out of sight.
Oh, who shall stand before the searching glance,
That knows all thought, the slightest form'd within
The secret soul of all assembled there ?
And all arraigns before the bar of truth
And holiness supreme, from whose behests
Evasion or appeal is ever vain !

The ransom'd have no fears.   The Book of Life
Is open, too, with all their names therein,—
The ledger of their claims—on what they stand,
And have a warrant for the place they fill ;
Its shining entries are a counterpart
To their experience,—the register
Of grace improv'd, and trial nobly borne,
And sin subdued, and holiness embrac'd :
The charter to their kingdom and their crown,
Upon each saint bestow'd, where each may read
His name thus seal'd, "God knoweth who are
    His ;"
His heart is voucher for its counterpart,
And has escap'd " from all iniquity."

    But, oh, what blanks are there !   What, not
        decern'd ?
Though long enroll'd by friendship's partial dream,
Among the ecstatic throng around the throne,

Withdrawn from spheres of usefulness and worth,
And witness-bearing for the truth of God,
And seeming zeal for the Redeemer's rights,—
Yet absent there, because that burning zeal
Was only mov'd by love of human praise,
And left no impress on the heart within
To trace its likeness in the Book of Life.
Some dearly lov'd, from whom a chilling breath
Or an uneasy throb we would debar,
Snatch'd from our side, we look beyond the clouds,
And are persuaded that the courts of bliss
And endless pleasure welcome their approach
To be enroll'd among the happy throng.
Alas ! we think not that no throbbings beat
In their cold hearts, harmonious with the strains
Of holy rapture ever swelling there.
Some gen'rous youth, whose unsuspecting heart
Sway'd pliant with the stream ; alike dispos'd
To vice or virtue, as it cross'd his path ;
Whose errors seem'd but the excess of joy.
Some lovely one, bedeck'd in female charms,
Elastic with emotion and delight ;
Whose peerless beauty, tenderness, and grace,
Darts like a sunbeam on the lover's heart ;
Grows faint and weary of this rude, rough scene,
And sinks into the grave.   Oh, can it be
That, unrecorded in the Book of Life,
Her fate beyond the grave is utter woe !

Whose are the absent names? My loving child,
On whom I doated with a quenchless love,
And long'd to see an honour'd child of God :
My bosom friend, assuager of my griefs,
Anxieties and cares : my neighbour, too,
Who shares the light that guides my heavenward
   way :
My fellow-man, who owns a deathless soul :
Oh, tell me where, in all that glorious roll,
May your own name be found? Not written
   there !
And you not horrified! Nay, still at ease,
And tripping lightly to the pit of woe ;
Or faintly trac'd, and scarcely to be seen,
Because not yet endors'd by your consent,
And made apparent by your willing deed.
Has blood incarnate lost its saving pow'r ?
Has love wax'd feeble ? Is its bosom fill'd ?
Has intercession fail'd, or weary grown ?
Is mercy all dried up ? Has sov'reign grace
Reserv'd no portion of its stores for you ?
Has this brief space, with its vain paltry cares,
Its fading pleasures and uncertain joys,
So crush'd the aspirations of the heart
That it is powerless to direct a wish,
Or make an effort to obtain the bliss
So freely proffer'd, yet so dearly won ?

   Will pride not stoop, a debtor to become

M

To sov'reign grace, for gifts of highest worth,
Yet be so mean as daily to accept,
Without return, the evanescent gifts
Which time contains from the same Donor's hand?
Or do you scorn to own so great a boon
From love divine, and boldly would prefer
To brave Almighty power, arous'd to wrath,
And meet perdition in its blackest form,
Than humbly crave a refuge not your own?
Oh, for an angel's trumpet to arouse
Your dormant spirit, e'er it be too late!
Oh, for the Spirit's power to touch your heart,
And make it yield submissive to his grace!

CHAPTER XVII.

ARGUMENT. — The Assembly before the Judgment Seat. —Who they are, and whence they come.—Their common Feeling. — Lost Salvation. — The Doom of Condemnation.—Responded to by all.—The Redeemed formally Acknowledged.—The sources of their Happiness. —Their Entry upon perpetually increasing Glory.

BEFORE the Throne and the Imperial Judge,
Invested with omnipotence and truth,
The teeming myriads of the human race,
By mandate irresistible, appear.
Reluctance is now paralys'd, and yields ;
Fear cannot skulk, nor hatred stay behind ;
All cavils are forgot, all pride succumbs,
And croaking infidelity is mute.
Without a plea resistance to support,
All generations come. From times remote,
Hid in the dust of ages pass'd away,
Without a trace left on the roll of time
To tell their era or the part they play'd ;
From recent date, fresh with the flush of life,
And stern debate amidst the world's rude strife,

Without a pause to smooth the plumage down,
And muster courage for the last account.

  The giant sons of hoar antiquity,
Who firmly walk'd beneath a load of years,—
Which modern dynasties can rarely boast,—
Whose iron sinews stoutly kept at bay
And baulk'd Death's onslaughts, till, with care
    mature,
They had devis'd their deep far-reaching schemes,
For consummation centuries beyond ;
These congregated with the remnant race
Of earth's exhausted, weak, degen'rate sons,
Who feebly sneak'd into vitality ;
Held a brief struggle with the wily foe,
Pass'd into evanescent manhood's sphere,
Laid hasty plans that in abortion sunk,
Or would not ripen in their paltry term
Of mortal state,—chid at their tardy growth,
And, disappointed, sunk into the grave.

  Earth's precious ones, ignoble or renown'd,
Who chose the wisdom of celestial climes,
Embrac'd its living principles of truth,
Imbib'd its spirit, grew into its form,
And were a part of holiness and love ;
The viewless seed hid in the inner life
Can never perish though creation fall,
But upward shoots to immortality.
Their study, where ?   Perhaps among the stars,

Whose countless number, magnitude, and spheres,
Their bright array, arrangement, and support,
Proclaim the vastness of the glorious source,
Whence the materials of their being sprung.
Perhaps 'mong lessons day to day imparts,
And night to night of wisdom's busy hand;
Among the pinions, pulleys, and cross wheels,
Which onward bear the doings of the world,
Whose adverse aims and jaring tendencies,
Drawn to a common, unseen end, reveal
Presiding goodness, power, beneficence,
Upholding, guiding, and controlling all;
Or in the marvels resident within,
The earnest student of the glorious whole,
Himself a world,—a race in miniature,
Peopled by thoughts and pregnant with design,
And indications of some parent source,
Which to discover fills the soul with peace;
Or in the waning light from Eden shed,
Held in tradition by the sires of men;
Or in symbolic or prophetic lore;
Or in historic page, writ by the pen
Dipt in celestial fire,—all pointing up
To Him who sits on the imperial throne.

  With willing minds, each had enough of light
To find a rock of everlasting strength,—
On it they rested, and on them the world;
It cannot fall to crush the humblest one

In whom the truth has found a safe retreat
From the deceptions of an erring race.
Earth's shining lights hung in the haunts of men,
Upon the heights and thoroughfares of life;
At pleasure's gates, and mammon's crowded doors;
In lowly vales of poverty and toil;
In sorrow's sombre halls; in light and shade;
Within the view of ev'ry wand'ring one,—
That he may see, and imitate, and live;
Or, if refusing, be without excuse.

They come elastic with foreshadow'd joy,
With felt salvation circling in their veins;
Their bosoms heaving with expectant bliss;
All sense, emotion, faculty, desire,
Girt with perennial youth, spontaneous burst
To bright experience of seraphic joy.
Peace sits triumphant upon ev'ry brow;
On ev'ry cheek tranquillity; Light beams
In ev'ry eye; Praise flows from ev'ry tongue;
In ev'ry heart is rapture, welling up
From utmost depths for high investiture
With immortality; while the deep springs
Of being, knit by viewless sympathy
And oneness indissoluble with Him
Who fills the throne august, draws them around
Within the essence of His full serenity,
Their deeds apparent to omniscient eye,
And pregnant with development, reveals,

With simultaneous voice, accepted worth,
Deriv'd from merit He on them conferr'd,
As guarantee of His acknowledgment.
The glorious throng all vacancy fill'd up;
And left no place for foes,—till, yielding more
To the attraction spirit-life well knows,
They cluster'd nearer to infinite love
And nestl'd in the folds of ecstacy.

Presiding pow'r conven'd another throng,
Crush'd and dejected with foreboding woe.
A wall of stern inflexibility,
And taintless holiness and love combin'd,
Rose up between the ransom'd and the lost.
All light within, all darkness round about,—
Like ancient bulwark of the chosen race :
So bright that ev'n despair might penetrate
And whet its anguish at the bliss foregone.
They come reluctant, cover'd with dismay,
Remorse and shame, and vile impenitence,
And guilt unpardon'd, and infernal hate,
Commingling into dooms unutterable.
The proof of guilt comes with them,—oozes out
In abject terror from the heart appall'd,
And ev'ry channel of intelligence ;
Conscience awakes in pangs, reticence fails,
And memory unfolds her hideous stores
In dark oblivion hid ; perception, sense,
And all volition, into terror urg'd,

In attestation shrink from the review.
Nor can they linger ; though the universe
Contains no spot so dreadful to approach.
Oblivion were bliss, perdition sweet,
And outer darkness a serene retreat,
Could it but veil the indignation hot
That from Omniscence ever on them pours.

No neutral ground is there, no midway state
By bliss disown'd, yet from despair secure,
Where indecision may convene her hosts,
And claim exemption from the scrutiny ;
No " sitters by," to scan and criticise,
With calm composure, the transactions there :
Each for himself appears, and is absorb'd
With the tremendous interests—all his own.
There Adam stands, pre-eminent in sin,
Who knew, as none else could, the two extremes
Of innocence and guilt ; who also mourn'd,
As none might do, his vile perfidious deed,
And refuge sought from the appalling storm,
In humble trust in the great Substitute,
And found it ample there,—abounding grace
To cover him,—to cleanse his guilt away,—
And bear him upward to unfading bliss.

His first-born, too, is there ; whose envious eye
First sate its passion upon human blood,
And gloated in revenge ; whose violence
First hurl'd a naked spirit to its doom,

Uncall'd by its great Sire.   The crimson mark
Pre-eminent appears upon him still,
Undimm'd by lapse of time, amidst the sum
Of deeds atrocious, impious, and vile,
Since then commuted, waiting their reward.
There, too, his victim, rudely scar'd to bliss ;
The first to fill a grave, or peer within
The deep unbroken solitude of death—
To thrust aside the dark mysterious veil
That shrouds celestial spheres from mortal view,
And gaze upon eternity's domain ;
Whose startl'd spirit, like a frighten'd bird,
Flew to the bosom of Omnipotence,
As a retreat from violence on earth ;—
The first sage student of a parent's light,
And deep experience of terrestrial things,—
Heaven's promise heard, and studied its import,
And rested on it in the hour of need.

There, too, Time's youngest child—last of the
  race,
That wail'd a mortal pang, and then withdrew—
Unconscious of the strife it had escap'd—
To spend existence in a happier clime.

And all between were there, of ev'ry race.
Long tenants of the tomb awoke to life
With those whose eyelids friendship scarce had clos'd;
The rude barbarian with the sage refin'd,
From Afric's burning sands, and India's plains,

And Lapland's icy shores, and Grecian isles ;
And Britain's favour'd land of light divine ;
And habitations dark of horrid cruelty,
In superstition sunk.   The savage rude,
Who roam'd the desert for a doubtful share
In life's repast, and the philosopher,
Who stunn'd the world with his discoveries ;
The peer and peasant stand on equal terms ;
The abject slave, whose lacerated back
Told in mute eloquence his many wrongs,
Confronts the master, of his pow'r despoil'd ;
Earth's potentates are there, of pomp depriv'd,
And all the trappings of inflated pride ;
There, too, her sons of toil, their labour hush'd,
And all its marts shut up.   Time's cares are gone,
Its trouble o'er, its burdens cast away,
The menial meets his lord ; the beggar mean
Stands on a par with despot of the world,
Nor shrinks abash'd at the comparison ;
The vulgar clown, whose light could scarcely guide
His erring footsteps to the way of peace,
Unblushing stands before the giant minds
That knew all science, save redeeming love—
Th' oppressor and oppress'd.   The martyr true,
And earnest witness for the truth divine,
Who rais'd his voice above the tempest fierce
Of human passion, avarice, and pride,
That oft o'erbore its gentle, pleading strains ;

Who dar'd to stand alone, and brave the storm ;
And by his blood attest its living pow'r ;
He meets once more with his inquisitor
Before another judge—their place revers'd ;
While truth rejected is the umpire stern,
Against whose dictate no appeal remains.

    The small and great are there.　Death has
      abjur'd
His ancient reign ; his victims are releas'd ;
His banquets ceas'd, and orgies at an end.
Time loads his boards no more.　War caters not—
His revenue is gone.　His gloomy cells
And dread reposit'ries are tenantless ;
The earth, the ocean, and the funeral pile
Have emptied all their stores ;—all have come forth,
Not one is absent from the great assize.

    Ponder, my soul ! there is a place for you.
On earth obscure, neglected, or despis'd,—
A vile excrescence on the social frame,—
Or lauded with applause, for princely deeds
And benefactions to your fellow-men ;
Unbias'd by circumstance, position, gifts,
Your everlasting fate of weal or woe
Is the fruition of your present state.

    One mighty theme engrosses ev'ry heart,
To the exclusion of all lesser thoughts.
The great salvation is now paramount ;
Seems what is ; meets with a full regard,

And will not be ignor'd ; is clearly seen
In all its native magnitude and worth,
As view'd by Him who wrought it out in time,
And now bestows it on His chosen ones.
Salvation won, or lost, reflects its hues,
In vivid colours, upon ev'ry cheek,
And thrills through ev'ry heart. The saints,
Already radiant with unclouded joy,
And full experience of unutter'd bliss ;
Above suspicion and the fear of guilt ;
From ev'ry charge releas'd ; from ev'ry stain
Now purified ; girt with celestial strength,
And buoyant with acknowledgment divine ;—
Exult in pregnant immortality.
While conscious guilt of deep persistent scorn,—
Of life reject'd, privilege despis'd,
And gifts abus'd, and offers all contemn'd,—
And all the tale of base ingratitude,
Impiety, and crime, with horror view'd
By memory acute, and understood
In light of proffer'd love, and pending doom,—
Already fills the wicked with dismay.
  Salvation lost ! Methinks the horrid shriek
Of felt damnation, heard above the storm
Of wrath unloos'd, and woe unutt'rable,
For ever surging in perdition's pit,
Would send a warning to respited earth ;
While Mercy waits, ere yet the utmost wail

Of outer darkness falls upon the soul,
That must be heard by all her wayward sons,
And force the most obtuse to flee and live.
  The eye recoils from the deep yawning gulf,
And shrinks from viewing the profound abyss.
So contemplation shudders to conceive,
Much less describe, the regions of despair.
Conception has no pencil to pourtray
The dread infliction of infinite wrath
Upon a finite soul.   Oh, how sustain
The smallest atom of the crushing load!
What seraph nearest to the throne
Of high intelligence, can estimate
One penal pang of the great Sacrifice,
In all its horror and intensity!
  Thence sum the whole e'er Justice was appeas'd ;
How mete it out in particles of woe,
Within the utmost of a creature's might ?
Oh, what of anguish would suffice to wipe
One stain from holiness, or chase away
One thought indignant from the Holy Mind ?
How pay arrears while still incurring more
By irremediable perversity ?
Ev'n though it were within the possible,
That far futurity contain'd some point
Absorbent of perdition and despair,
There is behind a load more grievous still,
In the rejection of a Saviour's love.

God's wrath endur'd, where is a refuge found
To hide the spirit from that love incens'd ?
But both combin'd, what agony unloos'd
Must prey for ever on the ruin'd soul ?
The frowning Judge with indignation arm'd,—
The dreadful sentence pregnant with despair,—
The self-upbraiding, unavailing grief,—
The bitter anguish and unutter'd woe,—
The gnawing worm,—the flaming tide of wrath,
That rushes ever through those dread abodes,—
Are terrible indeed. A brief respite,—
A hiding-place from the tremendous fate,
However mean, contemptible, or vile,—
Such insignificance as may conceal
The unsav'd spirit 'midst nonenity,—
Were worth ten thousand worlds. It cannot be !
Omniscience is not foil'd, nor yet deceiv'd ;
The humblest agent in persistent guilt
Must bear the doom his doings have incurr'd,
Whose every word strikes terror and despair—
" Depart from Me, ye cursed, to the pit ;
To everlasting, yet devouring, fire ;
Prepar'd for Satan and his rebel crew !"
Each spirit echoes the appalling doom,
And groans assent to its strict rectitude.
What it imports—its misery and woe—
O may I never, never, come to know !

    The doom pronounc'd, clouds of angelic hosts,

Who fill all space above, in deepest awe
And reverence profound, arrested, pause
In solemn view of their own finitude,
Amaz'd respond, and humbly harp, Amen.
And seraphs, hov'ring round the throne august,
Saw deep compassion blended with the ire
Of the Almighty Judge, that ting'd the doom
With anguish more acute, and in the depth
Of self-prostration humbly harp, Amen.
And shining armies spread through vasty space,
With views concentrate on the Mighty One,
Awaiting His behests of love or wrath,
Draw in the wing, and humbly harp, Amen.
And saints redeem'd obtain a clearer view
Of their demerit, danger, and escape,—
See what they might have been, and wond'ring why
A love so holy could find aught in them,
Or aught infuse, whereon it could repose,
To draw their being to a better fate,—
They nestle closer to that matchless love,
Evasive of the storm, and harp Amen.
And stricken spirits rushing in dismay
From burnish'd holiness,—in heart constrain'd
To vouch the justice of their dreadful fate,—
Preferring outer darkness and despair,
The full infliction of unutter'd woe,
To the tribunal of so pure a Judge,—
In consternation fleeing, shriek Amen.

The doom vibrated to the pit of woe,
And sent a thrill of horror, rage, despair,
More fierce and desp'rate through apostate hordes ;
And forc'd the flames of their dread prison-house
To ten-fold fervour and malignity,
That wrung a yell of acquiescent hate
From ev'ry outcast there—Amen, Amen.
Harmonious harps, in everlasting strains
Of Heaven's all-glorious spheres, as if reliev'd
From some vast crisis in th' imperial sway,
Spontaneous rose to melody sublime,
And universal shouts of boundless praise,
In tribute just to the Almighty Judge :—
" All blessing, honour, glory, wisdom, power,
Be ever His who sits upon the Throne !
Justice and judgment are His dwelling-place,
And all His ways are righteousness and truth."
Oh, for a seraph's eye to search around
The humblest base of Heaven's beatitude !
An heart to know, as deep experience may,
The unrestrain'd outflowing of the soul,
In all its perfect aptitude and strength,
To the vast fulness and complacency
That moves the bosom of Omnipotence
Towards the ransom'd, bought at such a cost !
All sight to gaze upon infinite love ;
All ear to hear the jubilate of Heaven !
All reason, wisdom, understanding, might,

To grasp in fuller measure and degree
The glorious raptures of unfading bliss ;
All tongue to praise, in everlasting strains
Of Heaven's own music, the infinite source.
What seraph highest in the courts above,
Most fully vers'd in its mysterious depths,
Can spy a limit in his vast survey ?
The wid'ning compass of His mighty span
Seems but to distance the unmeasur'd bounds.
Nay, but to taste one unalloy'd drop,
Pure from the ocean of infinitude ;
To feel one ray of certain glory, beam
Direct from the imperial throne into
The soul, appears security enough
Throughout the lapse of vast eternity.

But on the assembly of the ransom'd throng
The Judge's smile of glowing tenderness
And love serene benignantly repos'd,
In rest complacent, never to remove ;
And all His glory, dignity, renown,
As by Him purchas'd, and upon Him laid,
Encircled all,—gush'd into every heart,
As each could bear,—and made them one with
    Him.
They cluster'd deeper in His wondrous love,
Impelled by drawings of resistless grace,
And felt that love was Heaven at last secur'd.
Adoring angels, in astonishment,

N

Beheld the glorious throng absorb'd within
The massy folds of ravishment Divine,
That drap'd the essence of Emmanuel,
And round Him shed a halo of all praise,
Till now unutter'd in the realms of light ;
And still that throng had each a separate sphere,—
A hymn his own, and features all distinct,
And his own reasons for enraptur'd praise.
That praise was blended with seraphic song
On ev'ry note.　In thrilling unison,
Soft echo shed the welcome of the Judge,
In overpowering tenderness and love :
"Come ! of my Father blest ! To you belongs
The Kingdom long prepar'd.　'Tis now on you
Bestow'd in joint inheritance with Me."
　　With perfect knowledge, His omniscient eye
In satisfaction rested on each one.
In full possession of all perfect bliss,
He cast around them the enduring cords
Of everlasting, changeless, boundless love,
In bond perpetual of their high estate,
Such as at first, in measure and degree,
Had drawn them to Him by its winning charms,
But now unmeasur'd, save by the expanse
Of their exalted nature to receive.
It was the badge of His undoubted claim
To their peculiar praise, apart, distinct,
Yet toned to blend in unison sublime

With Heaven's seraphic melody ;
And through that bond such floods of rapture
  gush'd
Into their being and experience—
Such grateful sense of full security
And sweet repose, as angels cannot feel,
Who never pass'd through danger and alarm,
Nor knew aught less than pure unclouded bliss.
  Eternal fates unerringly dispens'd,
In strict accord, with rectitude and truth ;
Law vindicated, honour'd, and confirm'd,
And Heaven's supremacy more clearly prov'd,
By the decisions of the righteous Judge ;
Rebellion punish'd with its just deserts ;
Submission crown'd with purity and life.
The Judge arose in majesty supreme,
And light essential to the secret place
Of Great Jehovah, with the countless throng
Of His redeem'd, enclasp'd within the bond
Perpetual of His changeless love,
And with Him drew the bright seraphic tide
Of high intelligence, that fill'd all space
In adoration and astonishment
Round the judicial Throne.   Deep reverence,
And awe profound, and songs ineffable,
And highest praise, resounded through the spheres,
And simultaneous rose to holiest strains
Of loud hosannahs to the Lamb of God,

Upon His entrance to the halls of light,
With all the trophies of His matchless love,
Which louder peal'd and more ecstatic swell'd,
Till rapture shook the canopy of Heaven,
And burst the fonts of glory and renown,
And all the stores of unexplor'd delight,
And burst the pearly gates, and ingress made
For full admission of the Conqueror,—
Enrob'd with spirits rescued from the pit,
His spoils and captives wrested from the foe,
And with their shouts of everlasting praise,
And all their love, and gratitude, and joy,
And boundless influx of felicity,—
To reap the solace fulness ever craves ;
The luxury of pouring out His bliss
In copious floods into His ransom'd ones ;
To give each one a kingdom and a crown,
And regal sway, and all that these import,
And reign Himself the Head and King of all ;
Himself their sun, ensuring endless day ;
Their tree of life, with never-fading fruits ;
Their perfect fulness, pleasure, and delight ;
Their all in all while being endless rolls.

Within those realms of pure unclouded light
The Triune God, in majesty serene,
And love complacent, views the finish'd work
Of substitution,—it was ever view'd
In full completion by th' eternal mind,—

And rests with more ineffable delight,
And union more effulgent, on the Son,
To whom He gives, as their adored Head,
The custody entire, and access free,
To all the treasures resident in Him ;
To be diffus'd in copious floods on them,
Who, basking ever in the glorious light
Of immortality, feel bliss more sweet,
And rapture more intense, activity
In deep research, and full experience,
Amidst the doings of infinite love,—
Fraught with a brighter charm, contrasted with
The clouds and shadows of their mortal state.
In fulness of ineffable delight,
They cast their crowns adoring at His feet ;
For ever straining to a deeper depth,
And wider survey, and a loftier height,
Of that mysterious, boundless sov'reign love,
Which sought them out, and made them what
    they are.
As they advance, new raptures and delights
Urge to new songs of ecstacy and praise :—
   " Herein is love !—not love from us to Him,
But fervent love from Him,—on us bestow'd ;
That reach'd us, outcast, filthy, and deprav'd,—
That reach'd us sinking in the pit of woe ;
That would not be refus'd, nor turn'd aside,
Nor griev'd away by foul indignity,

Base unbelief, ingratitude, and sin ;
But sought and sav'd, and made us one with Him.
Oh, what is this ! that satiates all desire ;
Fills all conception, all volition draws ;
Absorbs all thought, all energy expands ;
Fires all emotion, ev'ry pow'r parvades
With perfect likeness to the glorious One !
What weight of glory insupportable
Is this, that fills all channels to the heart,
And clothes existence with beatitude !
No doubt assails to cast a transient shade
Upon the lustre of our high estate.
All, all is joy, unutterable delight ;
Intense surpassing rapture, peace, and joy,
Too crushing for weak finitude to bear.
Sustain us now, thou Spirit of all might !
Else we must perish with excess of bliss !"

To tell the dainties of the marriage feast,—
The luscious fruits and banquet ever spread,—
The matchless worth and dignity sublime
Own'd by Emmanuel, resident in Him ;
The gorgeous robes of righteousness most pure,
That drap'd the radiance of His chosen Bride ;
The glorious retinue of Heavenly hosts
In bright attendance ; all the golden harps,—
The strains immortal,—melodies sublime,
Which echo bore through spheres of Paradise,
For ever swelling and for ever new,

As being rolls through ages never clos'd,
Claims more than mortal aptitude and light.
  Ev'n thus the ransom'd of the Lord were
    brought
Into the presence of the great I Am,
To wander forth no more,—to sin no more ;
To toil and grieve, and bear the cross no more ;
Nor abject lie among time's filthy pots ;
To suffer pain, or doubt, or fear no more ;
To hope and trust, and utter prayer no more ;
All these are gone, and never can return ;—
'Tis glory now and pleasures evermore—
The full fruition of ecstatic bliss.
From out the throne life's river ever flows ;
All being there quaff immortality ;
Life deepens as they drink, and swells apace,
And brighter grows beside those living streams ;
Upon its banks the spreading tree of life
For ever blooms and drops its precious fruits ;
And as they feast, its nectarous delights
Inspires fresh vigour to their endless praise,—
Fresh admiration of the glorious One ;
Increasing ardour to their loud acclaim,
Which peals perpetual from the fragrant bow'rs
And shining verdure of unfading youth.
  Behold, He comes ! in faithfulness and truth,
With many crowns upon His glorious head,
And wounds of love all radiant on His brow ;

His bosom fill'd with all life's precious gifts,
For ever flowing to make Heaven blest ;
His raiment dazzling with essential light ;
And on His vesture vividly inscrib'd
His name, The King of kings and Lord of lords.
   Behold, He comes ! My soul, can you respond
With willing accents to the solemn peal,
And joyful cry, Ev'n so, Lord Jesus, come ?
Make haste, Belov'd ; be like a gentle roe,
Or loving hart, to bring me home to Thee ;
That I may join the ransom'd in the skies
In anthems ever new, and bright acclaim :—
" To Him that lov'd and wash'd us in His blood,
Who kings and priests hath made us unto God,
To Him let glory ever be.   Amen."

THE END.

CPSIA information can be obtained
at www.ICGtesting.com
Printed in the USA
BVHW041540310119
539155BV00010B/156/P